A New Vision for Human Resources

Defining the Human Resources Function by Its Results

D1468938

A NEW VISION FOR HUMAN RESOURCES

Defining the Human Resources Function by Its Results

JAC FITZ-ENZ
JACK J. PHILLIPS

CRISP Learning
Crisp Learning .com
Menlo Park, California

Editor-in-Chief: *William F. Christopher*

Project Editor: *Kathleen Barcos*

Editor: *LuAnn Rouff*

Cover Design: *Kathleen Barcos*

Cover Production: *Russell Leong Design*

Book Design & Production: *London Road Design*

Printer: *Phoenix Color Corp.*

Library of Congress Card Catalog Number 98-73103

ISBN 1-56052-488-X

03   10 9 8 7

CONTENTS

Preface

The human resources (HR) function has long been regarded as a necessary evil by many. Although in some companies this might have been a deserved reputation, it is not a fair characterization for the profession overall. Through a combination of executive management myopia and historic indifference, the function was originally populated by people who did not appreciate that they were part of a business establishment. They acted as though they were a social welfare agency. While they might have had good intentions, there was no way that they could have made a significant contribution.

Today, a growing group of sincere, business-minded professionals are determined to change the traditional view of the function. These people are the ones to whom this book is addressed.

In recent years, the cliché that people are our most important resource has actually come to mean something. Management now realizes that the last and clearly most effective leverage point in an organization is people. Nothing happens without people. Money, equipment, buildings, material . . . nothing happens until a human being acts. The human resources function now has the opportunity to move out of the background into the mainstream of organizational strategy and management. The key question is, can HR people step forward to take advantage of the chance? It does not matter if you are a one-person department or a member of a Fortune 100 human resources function. The principles of effective business management apply equally. Human resources should be, can be, and in many cases is, a valuable part of a business organization.

To move to the center of the organization, HR people must learn to talk in quantitative, objective terms. Organizations are managed with quantitative data. Unquestionably, at times managers make decisions based as much on emotion as fact. Nevertheless, day-to-day operations are discussed, planned and evaluated in hard data terms. The models, examples, descriptions and recommendations in this book are based on our over sixty years experience in human resources. We have worked with companies of all sizes on every continent except Antarctica. Although cultures and laws differ around the world, one thing remains constant. All business people live, think and talk in numbers.

If you, the reader, want to improve your ability to work with quantitative terms, we recommend that you start with a small number of important issues and develop measures for them. The reference section provides additional models and benchmark reports that can be your support tools. There is only one thing holding you and the rest of the human resources profession back from being a major player in tomorrow's marketplace. That is the will to be there. This book will help make you a more effective player in that market.

Good Luck.

I.

THE NEW VISION:
HUMAN CAPITAL MANAGEMENT

C USTOMERS, COMPETITORS, EMPLOYEES, TECH-
NOLOGY . . . everything is in flux. Customers
are becoming more demanding. Competitors
are growing more efficient and aggressive. Technology is
accelerating change and expanding everyone's capability.
Organizations are transforming themselves to survive in
the new marketplace. Work as we have known it has come
to an end.[1]

A new form is on the way that will require a totally
new approach to managing the human asset.[2] Given the
changes we are experiencing, it is difficult to imagine what
the world will be like even ten years into the future. One
thing is certain: What got us here, won't get us there.

In business we've stopped talking about personnel
administration or even human resources management.
Now we are dealing with the management of human
capital . . . and human resources is right in the middle of
it. It is no longer a cliché to say that people are the most
important asset of an organization. People are the only

dynamic asset. People are the causal force. Nothing happens without people. The human resources department's role is to help people be more effective in their work, as well as more satisfied. This effectiveness imperative is not measured in a flurry of programs. It is found in business results.

The Value Imperative

Every organizational unit affects business results. Each and every one absorbs resources, and produces services or products. Over the past two decades processes have been developed and tested for measuring staff as well as line function outputs. The methodology has proven to be valid and reliable. As a result, HR can now demonstrate how it contributes to the organization's service, quality and productivity (SQP) objectives. Service covers the interaction between the provider and the user or buyer. Service measurement is different than product measurement, even though both are aimed at meeting or exceeding the customer's requirements. Quality has to do with the number of errors or defects in either a service or a product. The quality people also usurped timeliness as one of their measures during the 1980s initial push for quality. Productivity is generally concerned with the cost and volume of products produced. However, it can also cover the outputs of a service unit. Ultimately, all business activities find their purpose in one or more of the SQP objectives.

Given the demand on organizations to compete or fail, every staff and line function must add value. The time has come for human resources to step forward and become more business focused. Since 1991, HR budgets have declined by 40% and staffing levels have shrunk by nearly 25%.[3] Increasingly, HR work is being delegated to the line, pushed out to transaction centers or outsourced. Paradoxically, this is very good news. It means that HR can spend less time on the nonvalue-adding administrivia, and more time working with line personnel to improve the operating efficiency of the organization. The central question is, *Is HR up to the challenge?*

The SQP Challenge

Service, quality and productivity (SQP). Improvements are the goal. They are interrelated, interdependent processes and results. Everything we do in an organization can be put into one of these three categories. All the management panaceas that come along should be judged by their ability to help managers and employees affect SQP. All proposals or requests for resources should be considered from the standpoint of how they will specifically improve SQP.

HR Gets into the Game

Thomas Watson, Sr., the man who turned IBM into one of the most successful companies in the world, said that business is a game, the greatest game in the world, if you know how to play it. Using his metaphor, consider how HR and the company resemble an athletic contest. Players populate the field. In this case, the players are the managers and employees of the company. They are the ones playing the very serious game of business.

Staff departments are in the locker room . . . under the stands. In the locker room they get ready to play the game. This is where they "suit up," get their equipment and ready their game plan. But if they want to score points, they have to leave the comfort and safety of the locker room and go onto the playing field. Once there, they see how the game is played and how the score is kept. In the Playing Field diagram (see Figure 1), we see that the players are members of the various line and staff functions.

Now consider how they score the game. In business, the score is kept in terms of service, quality and productivity results; all of which lead to financial returns. When

Functions	Productivity	Quality	Service	QWL*
Operations				
Producing	Units Built	Scrap Rate	On Time Shipment	Stress
Designing	New Products	Redraws	Acceptance	
Maintaining	Repairs	Breakdowns	Accidents	
Purchasing	POs Filled	Order Errors	On-time Arrivals	
				Morale
Sales/Marketing				
Selling	Units Sold	Margins	Customer Support	
Servicing	Calls Handled	Recall Rate	Problem Solved	
Market Research	Responsiveness	Data Utility	Customer Saved	Turnover
Advertsing/PR	Ads Designed	Copy Errors	Responses Handled	
Administration				Safety
Info Systems	Job Cost	Reruns	Faster Service	
Finance	Invoices	Billing errors	Clear Documents	
Planning	Plan On-time	Plan On-spec	Plan Clear	Satisfaction
Human Resources	Hiring Cost	Record Errors	Counseling Sessions	EAPs**

*QWL = Quality of Work Life
**EAPs = Employee Assistance Programs

Figure 1.   HR's playing field

4

HR leaves the safety of its locker room office and enters the field, it joins the game by working with the players from production, sales and marketing, and other functions to help them meet or exceed their SQP goals. If HR waits in the locker room for someone to call, it is essentially not in the game and can't complain if it is ignored or underfunded.

Aligning Human Resources with the Business

It has become a cliché to say that we must align the human resources function with the strategic business plan. What else should we align it with but the business plan? That statement, or goal, raises two important questions:

1. Precisely what does it mean to align the two?

2. If we accomplish alignment, will the HR staff be able to support the business plan?

Aligning HR with the strategic business plan starts by learning the goals of the plan. The goal of the business plan typically is to achieve certain profit objectives. In the case of not-for-profit organizations, the objective is to fulfill the mission of the organization. For the sake of simplicity, let's concentrate on profit as a goal.

There is a growing movement toward measuring the profitability of a company in terms of economic value added (EVA).[4] EVA is calculated as:

$$\frac{\textbf{Net Operating Profit After Tax}}{\textbf{Cost of Capital}}$$

A chain of events determines how well a company achieves EVA. To learn how to align HR with the strategic business plan we have to build a series of links that run backward from EVA to the HR department. At the end of that chain we will be able to determine what HR has to do to be aligned with and contribute to the objectives set out in the business plan. This linkage looks like the chain described in the following paragraphs. Alignment requires an unbroken connection from the beginning to the end of the chain: from EVA to staff responses and back again to EVA results.

The value chain works like this:

- **EVA,** or profit, is dependent on a company achieving competitive advantage in the marketplace.

- **Competitive Advantage.** Competitive Advantage simply means that your company does something better than the competition—as judged by the customers. If you have the lowest priced product, for the customer who seeks quality, you have no advantage. Competitive advantage is driven by being better in customer service, product quality or productivity, as measured in the average unit cost of the product or service. Starting in the early 1980s, American business jumped on the quality bandwagon. The goal was to reduce errors or defects in products and, later, services. A secondary goal was to reduce process cycle time, how long it takes to complete the total process. This contributed greatly to the efficiency of American industry and helped our companies win back market share that had been lost to foreign competitors, as well as compete domestically. The only failing of the quality movement was that it forgot about everything else. One of the forgotten "things" was, in some cases, the customer. So, while quality improved, competitive advantage did not always naturally follow.

- **Service–Quality–Productivity.** SQP is obtained by improvements that take place within the line and staff functions. When management is correct in choosing the service, quality, or productivity goal that matters most to the customer, the company usually gains a competitive advantage. The value of the competitive edge is that the company wins and holds more customers, leading to higher profit margins and a more stable growth pattern. This in turn attracts high-quality employees who are more likely to perform above average, which again drives SQP up, and the edge is sustained or continues to grow.

- **Line.** The traditional view is that the line adds value, while the staff is an expense. This is ridiculous. Why would anyone create a function that does not have a value-adding purpose? The issue is not that staff does not add value. It is that the value is harder to find than in the line function that directly makes or sells the product. In recent years it has become more apparent that staff departments can also be run as value-adding operations. The way they do this is to find out what the SQP objectives of the line functions are and then act directly to support them. There is a subtle but profound difference between staff programs or services and effects on line results.

- **Staff.** Accounting, human resources, information services and all other so-called staff functions add value when they link with the objectives of the line, providing just the right service at the right time and place and at a competitive cost. For example, if accounting processes invoices promptly and accurately, they contribute to the acceleration of cash flow. This provides funds to invest in better customer service, or new equipment to improve the product's unit cost. It is obviously adding value. When human resources designs a performance incentive plan and trains people, it contributes directly to improved customer service, product quality or unit cost by stimulating human motivation and building employee skills.

The key to finding HR's value contribution is to work backward from EVA or profit goals to desired competitive advantages such as increased market share. This will be obtained by meeting related service, quality or productivity objectives that are valued by the customers. Line functions hone their processes to achieve the SQP objectives. Staff departments contribute value when they partner with the line around the SQP objectives, connecting their services directly to the line through those objectives. When HR improves the delivery time, cost or quality of its services so that the line can meet its objectives, it is adding value. This connection can be traced back up the chain to EVA.

From Activity to Value Added

In the more successful organizations, HR's role is changing.[5] No longer does top management accept activity in place of value. On the one hand, HR still has to oversee its various administrative duties. It still must hire, pay, counsel and train people. Records have to be kept accurately. Processes have to run on time and be error-free. HR has to maintain the basic processes before it gets to have fun. But new technology and new structures are helping HR make the shift from administrivia to adding value. Following are some of the more popular approaches:

- Quality methods have helped with administrivia by simplifying processes

- Reengineering has shown a way to eliminate the unnecessary

- Technology allows for the delegation of some processes to line managers

- Benchmarking has shown examples of successful outsourcing

Nowhere is it written that the human resources department must personally handle every employee-related service. In short, there are many ways to throw off the shackles of administrivia while still fulfilling one's responsibility. When HR keeps the administrative wheels turning smoothly, it wins an opportunity to play a part in the running of the organization. This is the prerequisite to the new role.

Consulting, advising and partnering opportunities are present in most organizations. In fact, years of research and hands-on experience have proven that there is no barrier to HR playing those parts. If HR can show that it is a savvy, business-oriented group, it will find a position to play.

Value-Adding Skills

Playing a new role requires developing new skills. A fully functioning HR professional needs three types of skills today: *human resources management, business management and change management.* The Management Skills Checklist, (shown in Figure 2), outlines these requirements.

Human Resources Management

If you have been or are now employed in a human resources department, you probably have this first set of skills pretty well covered. If not, there are ample opportunities through job rotation, seminars and conferences to learn what you need to know. These skills of the profession are basic if you intend to function effectively at the program level for any length of time. However, they are not the key skills if you want to be a consultant or partner.

Business Management

Running a business is a complex, ever-changing affair. One of the most important skills one needs as a business manager is a sense of and appreciation for the strategic. Many staff people think at the program level

10

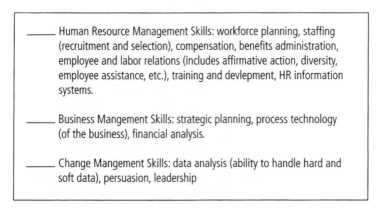

_____ Human Resource Management Skills: workforce planning, staffing (recruitment and selection), compensation, benefits administration, employee and labor relations (includes affirmative action, diversity, employee assistance, etc.), training and devlepment, HR information systems.

_____ Business Mangement Skills: strategic planning, process technology (of the business), financial analysis.

_____ Change Mangement Skills: data analysis (ability to handle hard and soft data), persuasion, leadership

Figure 2.   Management skills checklist

because they view their role as designers and administrators of human resource, finance or information system services. This inward-looking approach causes a disconnect between themselves and the managerial personnel who are trying to run a business enterprise. (It doesn't matter if the enterprise is for profit or not. All organizations must be managed.) HR professionals have to think strategically both in terms of human resource services and in terms of the direction, challenges and opportunities of the total enterprise. HR needs to think about the short- and long-term effects of various business initiatives. By understanding where top management is trying to take the business, HR can select, design, implement and manage its services more effectively.

Along with a strategic view, HR people need to know the basics of the business enterprise that employs them. Whether it is food processing, banking, healthcare, heavy manufacturing, electronic technology, government, education or any other endeavor, if you know what your business is about you can do a better job of supporting the people and helping to manage the human capital.

The third element is finance. This is where many HR people bow out. I'm not suggesting you become a CPA. But you can learn the basics of an income statement and a balance sheet in a two-day seminar. It is absolutely essential for everyone in an organization to understand the cash flow of the business. Cash underlies budgeting, staffing and operating. Without it there is no business. Understanding the fundamentals of accounting allows HR to discuss business problems from the same point of view, and using the same language, as its management colleagues.

Change Management

The new world marketplace is driving organizations through a continuous transformation in the struggle to remain competitive. As the primary guardians of the human capital of the organization, HR needs to learn how to manage change.

The first step is being able to diagnose or analyze what is happening. This means one has to be able to identify what type of data is needed, how to collect it and how to turn that data into useful information. Organizations are great collectors of human, financial and production data. The best organizations know how to use the data.

After discovering what needs to be done, you then have to influence, persuade or sell someone about your conclusions. All business is a constant negotiating process. Resources are limited, values differ, and goals and objectives sometimes conflict. An ability to persuade is essential for any person in an organization.

The third critical change management skill is leadership. It isn't enough to show what is happening and convince someone what needs to be done. You have to get into the game yourself if you expect to see your recommendations carried out. The skills of leadership have been described in countless books. There is also no shortage of material on change leadership.

Many human resource professionals need to improve their skills in the latter two categories. Once they learn how their organization operates, they can be more effective business partners. Keep in mind that line personnel do not care about HR programs. They are focused on meeting their own objectives. Furthermore, communication between line and staff is dependent on a common language. In business that idiom is quantitative. When HR learns the terminology of the company's financial statements, it can see precisely where and how it can contribute to operating improvements.

Business ROI Requirement

In competitive companies, every function is a value-adding operation. The marketplace is so intensely competitive today that each job must demonstrate an acceptable return on investment (ROI). Each must contribute in some way to continuous gains in product cost reduction, quality

levels and customer service. To show that HR is a contrib-
utor to those three business fundamentals, it needs a few
simple arithmetic formulas. While statistical proof is not
required, a focus on the connections between HR's activities and some positive, demonstrable business result is
imperative.

Five indicators are used to show the degree of change
that is taking place in the business. These measures of
change are: *cost, time, volume, errors and human reactions.*

- *Cost* covers the unit cost of a product or service. For
  each item produced, you can track its cost and how
  that changes as you work with people in the production units. You can also cost services. For example,
  what does it cost to handle customer inquiries on
  an average per-contact basis?

- *Time* is obviously a measure of the minutes, hours,
  days or weeks it takes to respond to a request for service, actually serve someone, or produce a product
  and ship it.

- *Volume* measurement is the amount of inputs and the
  amount of outputs, and the ratio of inputs to outputs.
  How many people does it take to produce a given
  amount of product, or serve a certain number of
  customers?

- *Errors* or defects is the ratio of defective items compared to acceptable items.

- *Human reaction* is the physical or emotional response
  that someone has to a service or product, or to the

way they are being treated. Most often this is measured in terms of customer reaction or employee attitudes or morale.

You will see these fundamentals of measurement in action in the Performance Measurement Matrix in Chapter 2. Keep them in mind as a mental model for categorizing the examples that follow in the rest of the book. Now let's move directly to applying ourselves to demonstrating how the human resources function can show the value it is contributing to the goals and objectives of the organization.

HR's Contribution

As human resources goes about its business of hiring, paying salaries, administering benefits and developing and retaining employees, it can apply simple quantitative terms to monitor changes in its results. This can include its internal costs, time to provide various services, amount of output generated from a given resource investment, level of work quality, and the satisfaction of the organization's employees and managers.

Many human resources people fear numbers. However, the fear is unfounded. Simple arithmetic functions—adding, subtracting, multiplying and dividing—will suffice. Heavy statistics are not necessary for reporting most business results. Statistical proof is not needed in business. Managers ask only for demonstrable evidence. Most people will accept a reasonably clear connection between what was done and the result of the activity.

HR's New Vision

Everyone needs a vision they can cling to through good times and bad. It is a foundation, a guide, a standard. A vision is a short version of a mission statement and it is more focused than a mission statement. It is a rallying point that can excite people. There are four good reasons for having a vision statement:

- To ensure clarity and consistency of purpose

- To provide a standard of reference for major decisions

- To inspire people

- To communicate to outsiders what you are about

What is your vision of the HR function? That is, what purpose does it serve? Why does your organization fund the HR department? In six words or less, write down the vision or purpose of the HR function—as it should be, not necessarily as it has been.

Your answer to the purpose statement should be focused on issues such as:

- Helping the organization meet its goals

- Adding tangible value

- Improving organizational effectiveness through people

Check your statement. The words are not the most important issue. The point is to focus everyone on contributing to the success of the organization.

- Does you statement list a number of tasks, processes or programs that HR is responsible for developing and maintaining? If it does, your focus is on activity. There is nothing wrong with activity, except that activity is expense. Doing something requires the commitment of resources—people, equipment and/or materials. Resources cost money. Everyone already knows how to spend money, so that is not a highly prized skill. Staff departments have traditionally been viewed and treated as expense centers. That is why they often have problems getting a large enough budget to do their job. It is also the principal reason why staff people are the first to be laid off whenever there is a downturn in the economy.

- Does your statement describe some results you want HR to achieve? Does it talk about contributing to the business goals? It may have included a descriptor of how it would do that (the activity), which is okay if a desirable result was included at the end. Does it allude to some type of value added? That is the key question. Once again, activity is expense. Results are value. If your statement is activity-focused, give it another try. If it is result-oriented, congratulations. You've passed the first test!

Conclusion

We all feel the tremendous rate of change that is taking place. It's evolutionary change at revolutionary speed. Never in recorded history has such widespread change affected so many people at such a rapid pace. To cope with that, organizations have had to change also.

When we are confronted with massive disruptions, the only feasible way to deal with them is to reassess fundamentals; in this case, the marketplace. Today, everyone in the world is playing in the same market. The challenge is to go back to service, quality and productivity as a benchmark. Anyone, in any organization that expects to be viable in the future, has to reassess his or her ability to provide excellent service, acceptable or better quality, at prices that customers will pay. HR has a role to play in this.

To play the game, HR has to get out of the locker room and onto the playing field. Instead of merely responding to requests for service, HR professionals have to become involved in the business process early on—at the strategy level. To win that position at the strategy table HR has to do two things:

- Shift from an activity focus to adding value

- Be able to demonstrate, in quantitative terms, that it is adding value.

The starting point is a vision of the purpose of the HR function as a value–adding operation. It is time to give up the activity game for the value game. This begins with creating a vision statement focused on value, and communicating that vision to all stakeholders inside and outside the department.

Once the vision is in place, a new skill set is required. The skills include not only the professional skills of human resource management, but also business and change management skills. Developing the business skills of strategic planning, process technology, and financial analysis is the first step to winning a seat at the management table. Once there, HR professionals need to manage change by collecting and analyzing data, developing persuasive arguments about the change needed, and then leading, or at least participating in, the change effort.

II.

MANAGING AND MEASURING HR

W E HAVE ALREADY DESCRIBED the three fundamental imperatives in business: improving service, quality, and productivity. Everything that everyone does should be aimed at making that happen. This applies to managing the human resources function as well.

- *Service* is the interaction between human resources and its internal customers, the managers, and the employees of the organization.

- *Quality* has to do with the rate of errors or defects in an HR service or product.

- *Productivity* is generally concerned with the cost and volume of HR products and services.

Management and Measurement Data

HR needs to generate hard data in order to know how well it is doing and where it needs to improve. Indeed, management begins with data collection.[6] Practically every management expert has told us that we can't manage what we don't measure. Without hard data to evaluate process efficiency and effectiveness, we are only overseeing a business unit not managing it. If we don't know what it costs, how long it takes or how much we have produced, how can we say we are managing something?

You will need three types of data in your measurement system: *customer satisfaction, process quality* and *productivity metrics*. You've already set it up with the vision statement you made in the last chapter. That told everyone what you are about, adding value in specific terms. The question of value is answered by the customer. Some customers want excellent service. Others demand top quality. Others buy based on best price. The successful company, and the successful human resources function, is the one that learns what the customer wants and then delivers it.[7]

Having recognized the three imperatives, now you can move to the corresponding three data collection steps. The most effective starting point is to contact your "customers" to find out how they feel about your current services. This can be done through surveys, interviews, focus groups or a combination of the three. You want to know two things. First, how much importance does your customer attach to each of your services? There is no point in continuing a service that the customer doesn't value. Second, along with importance is the level of satisfaction experienced by the customer. Following are typical services provided by an HR department:

Recruiting Process	Healthcare Insurance
College Recruiting	Profit-Sharing Program
Internal Job Posting	Employee Assistance Program
Supervisory Training	Employee Counseling Service
Technical Training	Award/Recognition Program
Management Development	Attitude Surveys
Wage and Salary Administration	Career Counseling/Development
Performance Appraisal System	Flexible Work Schedule
Incentive Pay Program	Personnel Records Access
Vacation/Holiday/Sick Leave System	Benefits Administration

Using subjective and objective information from its customers regarding service importance and satisfaction, the HR staff can decide what it needs to work on. Let's try it.

The Starting Point: Products and Services

The following exercise will give you a chance to build some experience in data collection. It shows you how easy it is and that there is no reason to fear either objective or subjective data. In fact, without data you simply cannot manage something proactively. Data takes you out of the locker room and prepares you to play the game.

Data Collection Exercise

1. Select a number of HR services that you perform. Choose from the preceding list and add to it any others that are important.

2. Make a rating scale of 5 or 7 points, such as the one shown here, giving it numerical values.

Service	Rating (Circle your rating number)						
	Low						High
‾‾‾‾‾‾‾	1	2	3	4	5	6	7
				Importance			
	1	2	3	4	5	6	7
				Satisfaction			
‾‾‾‾‾‾‾	1	2	3	4	5	6	7
				Importance			
	1	2	3	4	5	6	7
				Satisfaction			
‾‾‾‾‾‾‾	1	2	3	4	5	6	7
				Importance			
etc	1	2	3	4	5	6	7
				Satisfaction			

3. Place one of the services to the left of each set of scales.

4. Write instructions asking people to review the service and respond by circling the number that most closely indicates their view.

5. Pass out the questionnaire to as large a number of managers and employees as you can.

6. Collect the questionnaires and average the scores for each service.

7. A satisfaction score 2 or more points below the importance score indicates a significant problem, provided the importance score is 5 or above.

How Well Do You Deliver?

Along with knowing the state of your products and services as seen by your customers, you also need to know how they view your delivery methods. In the service business, often delivery is as important as the service itself. Here are a few considerations to use for starters:

- Handling of confidential matters

- Quality of the advice you give the customers

- Responsiveness to customer requests

- Reliability of your unit's performance over time

- Readability of your materials

- Professionalism of your staff

- Your ability to anticipate and prepare customers for the future

- Concern for customer problems

- Ease of use of your processes

- Quality and quantity of information available and communicated to customers

- Knowledge of the customer's business

- Ability to help the customers achieve their objectives (this is your contribution)

Ask your customers to score your performance on a 1 to 7 point scale, with seven (7) being highest, on a set of service delivery behaviors. Use the same method you used with the products and services. Don't forget to ask about both importance and satisfaction.

The Next Step: Process Quality Improvement

Once you have your data in hand, you can decide what needs attending to and what you are excelling at. You might know what to do to improve the service, product or process. One way to deal with customer dissatisfaction is to simply respond with the service or product that they ask for or improve the delivery method. However, that might not be possible. Some problems are complex and do not lend themselves to simple solutions. This takes you to the next step, which is gathering data on your process. You can look inside the organization for someone else who is rendering a similar service. Or you can benchmark high-performing HR departments in other companies.

Benchmarking can be an effective idea generator. You can find out how the top performers do it. One caution: Be careful before adopting what another company is doing. Their success can be your disaster. You need to understand their culture and problems before you copy their solution. It is best to look behind their process to why they did what they did. Will that work for you in your company? When you have a clear solution in mind, you can begin planning its implementation.

The Last Step: Metrics

Finally, you are ready to respond. Now all you need is a set of performance targets—return on investment goals. After all, you have to know where you are, where you are headed, and what it will look like when you get there. Without performance metrics, you leave yourself vulnerable to those who would say after the fact that you didn't achieve anything of value. To prepare your evidence you need quantitative data. Here's where measurement becomes imperative.

Comparative benchmark data is very helpful in setting your goals. How are others, those you benchmarked for processes or another group of comparable firms, doing in these areas? You might find that you are among the best in the business already. This fact can be communicated to management. If you aren't the best, is it because of lack of budget or staff, staff skill deficiencies, or what? Again, you may be able to use the benchmark data to obtain the resources you need to improve your service.

Change Measurement

Recall the five indicators used to show the degree or amount of change that is taking place in levels of service, quality or productivity: cost, time, quantity or volume, errors and human reactions.

- **Cost** covers the unit cost of the product or service. For each item produced, you can track its cost and how that changes as you work with people in the production units. You can look at the cost per hire, cost per trainee, or cost per paycheck. You can also track the cost of a service. For example, what does it cost to handle employee problems on an average per-contact basis?

- **Time** is obviously a measure of the minutes, hours, days or weeks it takes to respond to a request for a service or product, actually serve someone or produce a product, and ship it. Time to fill jobs, prepare and deliver a new training program, evaluate jobs or counsel employees can be monitored.

- **Volume** is often viewed in productivity terms–the ratio of inputs to outputs. How many people does it take to fill jobs, produce paychecks, process benefit claims, or design and conduct a training program?

- **Errors** or defects is the ratio of defective items to acceptable items. This can include the rate of errors in employee records. Or it could be a measure of the quality of new hires. Accuracy of reports is another quality measure.

- **Reaction** is the physical or emotional response that someone has to your service or product, or to the way they are being treated. Most often this is measured in terms of customer satisfaction or employee attitudes or morale.

We can put the results and change measures together in a matrix for ease of understanding and communicating. This matrix can be overlaid on any function, because all jobs and business units aim to improve SQP objectives, and measure them in one or more of the five indicators. It is good practice to look for more than one way to measure change. For example, if you show that you have successfully reduced the cost of hire, someone might say "Yes, but the quality of the new hires is declining." Or they could comment that it is taking too long. So, before reporting a result, look at cost, time, volume and quality indexes. The human reaction is the response you get to your work. In the performance matrix (see Figure 3), some of the cells have been filled in for human resources services. These are just a few examples to stimulate your imagination. Keep in mind that the objective is always to show a positive, quantitative return on investment in human resource services.

	Service	Quality	Productivity
Cost			Unit Cost (cost per hire)
Time		Time to Respond (time to fill jobs)	
Volume			Amount Produced (number of checks out)
Errors		Defect Level (employee file errors)	
Human Reactions	Customer Satisfaction (hiring manager reaction)		

Figure 3. Performance measurement matrix

A Measurement Exercise

In the matrix shown in Figure 3, one example has been shown for each of the five indexes and each of the three SQPs. Try to fill in more of the cells. Consider all the things HR produces in hiring, paying, benefits administration, employee relations, training and information processes. How many cells can you fill?

1.   Photocopy and enlarge the blank performance matrix, shown in Figure 4. Use one copy per HR function.

2.   Fill in as many cells as you can with measures that come to mind. Don't worry about how practical they are. Just go for volume now.

	Service	Quality	Productivity
Cost			
Time			
Volume			
Errors			
Human Reactions			

Figure 4.   Performance measurement matrix

With customer service, process quality and performance metrics, HR staffs can plan, act and evaluate their performance. Then, they can recycle the process and do it over. This is a continuous improvement process that everyone can understand and work toward.

Conclusion

You now have a model from which to consider specific measurement situations. You know what is important to you and your customers. This is a launching point as well as a reference for later consideration.

The following four chapters give you more in-depth examples and applications of measurement across a wide variety of situations. As you work through succeeding chapters, you will think of more measures. Keep the blank form handy and come back to it from time to time to add new measures. In the end, we expect that you will find many ways to demonstrate the value you are contributing to your organization.

III.

COLLECTING DATA TO MEASURE THE HR CONTRIBUTION

M EASURING THE HUMAN RESOURCES contribution requires collecting a variety of data at different times to assess the status of a specific activity, program, initiative, or function within HR. This chapter highlights the different ways to collect data, beginning with the types of data and the overall evaluation framework. While several macro measures can be monitored which reflect the success of the overall HR function—such as absenteeism, turnover, and job satisfaction—it is often more useful to measure the success of new programs or initiatives designed to improve these measures. For example, it may be helpful to know:

- The success of a new recruiting process

- The savings from a more efficient employment procedure

- The return on investment in a new gainsharing program

- The reaction to changes in the employee benefits package

- The impact of a new diversity initiative

- The effectiveness of a newly revised orientation process

- The payoff of a management development program

- The contribution of an employee suggestion program

- The financial benefits of a sexual harassment prevention program

The frame of reference for many evaluation strategies is to measure the success of a new program or initiative. The variety of programs or activities listed above requires a wide range of data collection techniques, all described in this chapter.

Preliminary Issues

Before describing specific data collection methods, two preliminary issues need to be defined and described. These involve the different levels of evaluation and the types of data collected.

Levels of Evaluation

The concept of different levels of evaluation was developed almost forty years ago by Kirkpatrick.[8] Figure 5 shows the five-level framework used in this book. At Level 1, *Reaction,* satisfaction from HR program participants is measured. Almost all organizations evaluate at Level 1, usually with a generic questionnaire.

At Level 2, *Learning,* measurements focus on what participants learned as a part of the HR program. Measures are taken from tests, skill practices, role plays, simulations, group evaluations, and other assessment tools. A learning check is helpful to ensure that participants have absorbed the HR program material and know how to use it. At Level 3, *Implementation,* a variety of follow-up methods are used to determine if participants applied what they learned and implemented the HR program. Implemen-tation is a critical element in a program's success, and a Level 3 evaluation uncovers problems and barriers as well as progress and enablers. At Level 4, *Business Impact,* the measurement focuses on the actual business results achieved with the program. Typical categories for Level 4 measures are output, quality, costs, time and customer satisfaction. At Level 5, the ultimate level of evaluation, *Return on Investment,* the measurement compares the program's monetary benefits to the program costs. Although the ROI can be expressed in several ways, it is usually presented as a percent or benefit/cost ratio. For a comprehensive evaluation, the cycle is not complete until the Level 5 evaluation is conducted.

For some HR efforts a reaction evaluation is sufficient. The various stakeholders may only need to know the reaction from employees regarding a specific HR initiative. Sometimes it is important to measure learning as intellectual capital. Knowledge management and the learning organization become critical concerns. In other situations, it is important to know how HR processes, programs and initiatives are actually functioning as they are implemented. Implementation measures are necessary in almost every new program. Still, in other situations, it is necessary only to monitor business impact measures, such as the number of grievances, absenteeism and turnover. These measures are often monitored routinely and compared with historical values.

Very few organizations actually conduct evaluations at the ROI level. This may be because ROI evaluation is often characterized as a difficult and expensive process. Although business results and ROI are desired, it is very important to evaluate the other levels. In some HR programs, a chain of impact should occur when skills and

Level	Brief Description	Example-Positive Displine Program
1. Reaction	Measures participant's reaction to the HR program or initiative.	Employee satisfaction with program
2. Learning	Measures skills, knowledge, or attitude changes	Knowledge of policy; skills of supervisor
3. Implementation	Measures changes in behavior on the job and specific applications of a HR program or initiative	Application of policy: change in employee habits
4. Business Impact	Measures business impact of the HR program or initiative	Reduction in absenteeism and grievances
5. Return on Investment	Compares the monetary value of the results with the costs for the HR program or initiative, usually expressed as a percentage	ROI from program expressed as percentage

Figure 5.   Characteristics of evaluation levels

knowledge learned (Level 2) are applied on the job as the HR program is implemented (Level 3) to produce business results (Level 4). If measurements are not taken at each level, it is difficult to conclude that the results achieved were actually caused by the HR program. Because of this, it is recommended that evaluation be conducted at all levels when an ROI evaluation is planned.

Sorting Out Hard and Soft Data

When collecting data, many organizations find it helpful to divide data into hard and soft categories. Hard data is the traditional measure of organizational performance, as they are objective, easy to measure and easy to convert to monetary values. Hard data is often a very common measure. Data has high credibility with management, and is available in every type of organization.

Hard data represents the output, quality, cost and time of work-related processes. Figure 6 shows a sampling of typical hard data under these four categories. Almost every department or unit will have hard data performance measures. For example, a government office approving applications for work visas in a foreign country will have these four measures among its overall performance measurement: the number of applications processed (output), cost per application processed (cost), the number of errors made processing applications (quality) and the time it takes to process and approve an application (time). Ideally, HR programs for employees in this unit should be linked to one or more hard data measures.

Output	Time
Units Produced	Equipment Downtime
Tons Manufactured	Overtime
Items Assembled	On Time Shipments
Items Sold	Time to Project Completion
Forms Processed	Processing Time
Loans Approved	Supervisory Time
Inventory Turnover	HR Time
Patients Visited	Meeting Scheduals
Applications Processed	Repair time
Students Graduated	Efficiency
Productivity	Work Stoppages
Work Backlog	Order Response
Shipments	Late Reporting
New Accounts Opened	Lost Time Days

Costs	Quality
Budget Variances	Scrap
Unit Costs	Waste
Cost by Account	Rejects
Variable Costs	Error Rates
Fixed Costs	Rework
Overhead Costs	Shortages
Operating Costs	Product Defects
Number of Cost Reductions	Deviation from Standard
Project Cost Savings	Product Failures
Accident Costs	Inventory Adjustments
Program Costs	Time-Card Corrections
Sales Expense	Percent of Tasks Completed Properly
	Number of Accidents

Figure 6.   Examples of hard data

Because many HR programs are designed to develop soft skills, soft data is needed in evaluation. Soft data is usually subjective, sometimes difficult to measure, almost always difficult to convert to monetary values and behavior-oriented. When compared to hard data, soft data is usually less credible as a performance measure. Soft data items can be grouped into several categories; Figure 7 shows one such grouping. Measures such as employee turnover, absenteeism and grievances appear as soft data items, not because they are difficult to measure, but because it is difficult to accurately convert them to monetary values.

Questionnaires and Surveys

Probably the most common form of data collection method is the follow-up *questionnaire*. Ranging from short reaction forms to detailed follow-up tools, questionnaires can be used to obtain subjective information about participants, as well as to objectively document measurable business results. Versatile and popular, the questionnaire is the preferred method for capturing Level 3 and 4 data in some organizations.

Surveys represent a specific type of questionnaire offering several applications for measuring the success of HR programs. Surveys are used in situations where only attitudes, beliefs and opinions are captured; whereas, a questionnaire has much more flexibility, capturing data ranging from attitudes to specific improvement statistics. Surveys can have Yes or No responses when an absolute agreement or disagreement is required, or a range of responses may be used—from "strongly disagree" to "strongly agree." A five-point scale is very common.

Work Habits	New Skills
Absenteeism	Decisions Made
Tardiness	Problems Solved
Visits to the Dispensary	Conflicts Avoided
First-Aid Treatments	Grievances Resolved
Violations of Safety Rules	Counseling Success
Communication Breakdowns	Listening
Excessive Breaks	Reading Speed
Follow-Up	Intention to Use New Skills
	Frequency of Use of New Skills
Work Climate	**Development/Advancement**
Number of Grievances	Number of Promotions
Number of Discrimination Charges	Number of Pay Increases
Employee Complaints	Number of HR Programs Attended
Job Satisfaction	Requests for Transfer
Employee Turnover	Performance Appraisal Ratings
Litigation	Increases in Job Effectiveness
Attitudes	**Initiative**
Favorable Reactions	Implementation of New Ideas
Attitude Changes	Successful Completion of Projects
Perceptions of Job Responsibilities	Number of Suggestions Implemented
Perceived Changes in Performance	Setting Goals and Objectives
Employee Loyalty	
Increased Confidence	

Figure 7. Examples of soft data

A questionnaire may contain any or all of several types of questions, including open-ended, checklist, two-way, multiple choice, ranking and matching.

One of the most difficult tasks is determining the specific issues to address on a follow-up evaluation questionnaire. Some possibilities for capturing both Level 3 and 4 data are:

- Progress with objectives

- Action plan implementation

- Relevance of program

- Use of program materials

- Knowledge/Skill enhancement

- Skills used

- Changes with work

- Improvements/Accomplishments

- Monetary impact

- Confidence level

- Improvements linked with program

- Investment perception

- Linkage with output measures

- Barriers

- Enablers

- Management support

- Other solutions

- Target audience recommendations

- Suggestions for improvement

Obviously, asking *all* of these questions could cause the response rate to be reduced considerably. The challenge, therefore, is to tackle questionnaire design and administration for maximum response rate. This is a critical issue when the questionnaire is the primary data collection instrument and most of the evaluation hinges on the questionnaire results. The following actions can be taken to increase response rate:

- Provide advance communication

- Communicate the purpose

- Explain who will see the data

- Describe the data integration process

- Keep the questionnaire as simple as possible

- Simplify the response process

- Utilize local manager support

- Let the participants know they are part of the sample

- Consider incentives

- Have an executive sign the introductory letter

- Use follow-up reminders

- Send a copy of the results to the participants

Collectively, these items help boost response rates to 50–80%, even with lengthy questionnaires that might take thirty minutes to complete.

Using Interviews and Focus Groups

Another useful data collection method is the *interview*. Interviews can be conducted by the HR staff, the participant's supervisor or an outside third party. Interviews can secure data not available in performance records, or data difficult to obtain through written responses or observations. Also, interviews can uncover success stories that can be useful in communicating evaluation results. Participants who may be reluctant to provide input in a questionnaire will often volunteer the information to a skillful interviewer who uses probing techniques. While the interview process uncovers changes in behavior, reaction, and results, it is primarily used with Level 3 data. A major disadvantage of the interview is that it is time-consuming. It also requires that HR prepare interviewers, to ensure that the process is consistent.

Interviews usually fall into two basic types: structured and unstructured. A structured interview is much like a questionnaire. Specific questions are asked, with little room for deviation from the desired responses. The primary advantages of the structured interview over the questionnaire are that the interview process can ensure that the questionnaire is completed and that the interviewer understands the responses supplied by the participant.

The unstructured interview allows for probing for additional information. This type of interview uses a few general questions, which can lead into more detailed information as important data is uncovered. The interviewer must be skilled in the probing process.

An extension of the interview, the *focus group* is particularly helpful when in-depth feedback is needed for a Level 3 evaluation. The focus group involves a small group discussion conducted by an experienced facilitator.

It is designed to solicit qualitative judgments on a given topic or issue. All group members are required to provide their input, as individual input builds on group input.

The focus group technique has several advantages. The basic premise of using focus groups is that when quality judgments are subjective, several individual judgments are better than one. The group process, in which participants often motivate one another, is an effective method for generating new ideas and hypotheses. It is inexpensive and can be quickly planned and conducted. Its flexibility makes it possible to explore an HR program's unexpected outcomes or applications.

Observation

Another potentially useful data collection method is *observing participants* and recording any changes in behavior. The observer may be a member of the HR staff, the participant's supervisor, a member of a peer group, or an outside party. The most common observer, and probably the most practical, is a member of the HR staff.

Five methods of observation can be utilized, depending on the circumstances surrounding the type of information needed:

- A behavior checklist for recording the presence, absence, frequency, or duration of a participant's behavior as it occurs.

- A delayed report method in which the observer does not use any forms or written materials during the observation. The information is either recorded after the observation is completed or at particular time intervals during an observation.

- Video recording of behavior in every detail.

- Audio monitoring of conversations of participants who are using the skills.

- Computer monitoring of employees who work regularly with a keyboard.

Observation is often misused or misapplied to evaluation situations, causing some to abandon the process. The effectiveness of observation can be improved when observers are fully prepared. The process is systematic, and the observers' influence is minimized.

Monitoring Performance Data

Monitoring performance data enables management to measure performance in terms of output, quality, costs, and time. In determining the use of data in the evaluation, the first consideration should be existing databases and reports. In most organizations, performance data suitable for measuring the improvement resulting from an HR program is available. If not, additional record-keeping systems will have to be developed for measurement and analysis. At this point, as with many other points in the process, the question of economics enters. Is it economical to develop the record-keeping system necessary to evaluate an HR program? If the costs are greater than the expected return for the entire program, then it is meaningless to develop them.

Existing performance measures should be thoroughly researched to identify those related to the proposed objectives of the program. Several performance measures may be related to the same item. For example, the efficiency of a production unit can be measured in a variety of ways:

- Number of units produced per hour

- Number of on-schedule production units

- Percent utilization of the equipment

- Percent of equipment downtime

- Labor cost per unit of production

- Overtime required per piece of production

- Total unit cost

Each of these, in its own way, measures the efficiency of the production unit. All related measures should be reviewed to determine those most relevant to the HR program.

In some cases, data isn't available for the information needed to measure HR effectiveness, and the HR staff must help develop record-keeping systems, if this is economically feasible. In one organization, a new employee orientation system was implemented on a company-wide basis. Several measures were planned, including early turnover representing the percentage of employees who left the company in the first six months of their employment. An effective employee orientation program should influence this variable. At the time of the program's inception, this measure was not available. When the program was implemented, the organization began collecting early turnover figures for comparison.

Developing new measures usually involves other departments or a management decision that extends beyond the scope of the HR department. The administration department, the operations division, or the information technology section may be instrumental in helping determine if new measures are needed and, if so, how they will be collected.

Action Plans and Performance Contracts

The *action plan* contains detailed steps to accomplish specific objectives, and is a common type of data collection method. With this approach, participants are required to develop action plans as part of an HR program. The plan is typically prepared on a printed form.

The action plan shows what is to be done, by whom, and the date it should be accomplished. The action plan approach is a straightforward, easy-to-use method for determining how participants will change their behavior on the job and achieve success with the HR program.

The development of the action plan requires two tasks: determining the areas for action, and writing the action items. Both tasks should be completed during the program. The areas for action should originate from the content of the program and, at the same time, be related to on-the-job activities. A list of potential areas for action can be developed independently by participants, or a list may be generated in group discussions. The list may include an area needing improvement, or represent an opportunity for increased performance.

The topic selected should be stated in terms of one or more objectives, which should state what is to be accomplished when the contract is complete. These written objectives should be understandable by all involved, challenging, achievable, largely under the control of the participant, and measurable and dated.

It is usually more difficult to write the specific action items than it is to identify the action areas. The most important characteristic of an action item is that it be written so that everyone involved will know when it occurs.

The action plan process should be an integral part of the HR program and not an add-on or optional activity. To gain maximum effectiveness from action plans, and to collect data to measure business impact and ROI, the following steps should be implemented:

- Communicate the action plan requirement early.

- Describe the action planning process at the beginning of the program.

- Teach the action planning process.

- Allow time to develop the plan.

- Have the coordinator/facilitator approve the action plans.

- Require participants to assign a monetary value for each improvement.

- Require action plans to be presented to the group, if possible.

- Explain the follow-up mechanism, timing, and requirements.

- Ask participants to isolate the effects of the HR program, after the evaluation period.

- Ask participants to provide a confidence level for estimates.

- Collect action plans at the predetermined follow-up time.

- Summarize the data and calculate the ROI.

If developed properly, each action plan should have annualized monetary values associated with improvements. Also, each individual should indicate what percent of the improvement is directly related to the program. Finally, each participant should provide a confidence percentage, reflecting the uncertainty with the process and the subjective nature of some of the data that may be provided. Adjustments during the analysis make the process very credible.

The *performance contract* is essentially a slight variation of the action planning process. It is a written agreement between a participant and the participant's supervisor (and sometimes an HR staff person). The participant agrees to improve performance in an area of mutual concern related to the HR program. The agreement is in the form of a project to be completed or a goal to be accomplished soon after the program is completed or operational. The agreement spells out what is to be accomplished, at what time, and with what results. The process of selecting the area for improvement is similar to the process used in the action planning process.

Selecting the Appropriate Method

This chapter has presented several methods to capture data to evaluate an HR program. Collectively, they offer a wide range of opportunities to collect data in a variety of situations. Several issues should be considered when deciding which method is appropriate for a situation, including type of data, time required, costs, accuracy, utility and disruption of work.

The method should be matched with the type of data. Surveys and questionnaires can capture implementation data (Level 3) and business impact data (Level 4). Observation, interviews, and focus groups are more appropriate for implementation data (Level 3), while action planning and performance contracting can capture both Level 3 and Level 4 data. Performance monitoring, by definition, collects business impact data (Level 4).

Conclusion

This chapter presents the concept of evaluation levels, which provides a useful framework for developing a comprehensive HR measurement and evaluation process. The different types of data, classified as hard and soft, are defined and described along with the most common methods for collecting both types of data. A comprehensive HR measurement and evaluation system will use a variety of techniques to collect both types of data for HR programs, activities, and functions.

IV.

ISOLATING THE EFFECTS OF HR PROGRAMS AND INITIATIVES

T HE FOLLOWING SITUATION is repeated often: A significant increase in an important business performance measure is noted after a major HR program is implemented, and the two events appear to be linked. The HR vice president makes this connection in a presentation to senior executives. A key manager asks, "How much of this improvement was actually caused by the HR program?" When this potentially embarrassing question is asked, it is rarely answered with any degree of accuracy and credibility. While the change in performance may be linked to the HR program, other factors usually have contributed to the improvement. This chapter explores useful strategies for isolating the effects of the HR programs. These strategies are utilized in some of the best organizations as they attempt to measure the return on investment in human resources.

Identifying Other Factors: A First Step

As a first step in isolating HR's impact on performance, identify all of the significant factors that may have contributed to the performance improvement. This step communicates to interested parties that other factors have influenced the results, underscoring the premise that the HR program is not the sole source of improvement. Consequently, the credit for improvement is shared with several possible variables and sources, an approach that is likely to gain the respect of senior management.

The potential sources for identifying major influencing variables are:

- The client

- Program participants

- HR program analysts and developers

- Supervisors, managers and executives

Taking time to focus attention on all variables that may have influenced performance brings additional accuracy and credibility to the process. It moves beyond the scenario in which results are presented with no mention of other influences, a situation that often destroys the credibility of an HR impact study.

Using Control Groups

The most accurate approach for isolating the impact of HR is the use of control groups in an experimental design process.[9] This approach uses an experimental group that is involved in the HR program and a control group that is not. The composition of both groups should be as similar as possible and, if feasible, the selection of participants for each group should be made randomly. When this is possible and both groups are subjected to the same environmental influences, the difference in the performance of the two groups can be attributed to the HR program.

The control group and experimental group do not necessarily need pre-program measurements. Measurements are taken after the program is implemented, and the difference in the HR performance measure of the two groups shows the amount of improvement that is directly related to the program.

Control group arrangements appear in many settings. In a large finance company with 800 branches, a new branch manager selection program was implemented using a control group arrangement.[10] One-third of the branches served as the experimental group while the other two-thirds served as the control group. In this arrangement, the success of the program, measured by reduction in turnover, was determined by comparing the control group with the experimental group. The results were phenomenal and ultimately yielded a 2,000% return on investment for the HR program.

The use of control groups may create the perception that the HR staff is creating a laboratory setting, which can cause a problem for some executives. To avoid this stigma, some organizations run a pilot program using pilot participants as the experimental group and not informing the nonparticipating control group. In this arrangement, it is important for the pilot group to be matched with the control group to the fullest extent possible to allow a comparison of the two groups. In practice, most new programs are implemented on a pilot basis, thus creating the possibility for a control group arrangement. The challenge is to consider this process early, before a pilot group is actually selected, so that the variables can be identified to match the two groups.

The control group process does have some inherent problems that may make it difficult to apply in practice. The first major problem is the selection of the groups. From a practical perspective, it is virtually impossible to have identical control and experimental groups. Dozens of factors can affect employee performance, some of them individual and others contextual. To tackle the issue on a practical level, it is best to select three to five variables that will have the greatest influence on performance, and use them as a basis for identifying the two groups.

Another problem is contamination, which can develop when participants in the HR program explain the process to others who are in the control group. Sometimes the reverse situation occurs when members of the control group seek information from the experimental group. In either case, the experiment becomes contaminated as the influence of the HR program is passed on to the control group. This can be minimized by ensuring that control groups and experimental groups are at different locations, have different shifts, or are on different floors in the same building. When this is not possible, sometimes it is helpful to explain to both groups that one group will be involved in the program now and another will be involved at a later date. Also, it may be helpful to appeal to the sense of responsibility of those in the HR program and ask them not to share information with others.

Because this is an effective approach for isolating HR, it should be considered as a strategy when the impact of a major program or initiative is planned. It is important that program impact be isolated with a high level of accuracy, the primary advantage of the control group process.

Trend-Line Analysis

Another useful technique for approximating the impact of HR is trend-line analysis. With this approach, a trend-line is drawn, using previous performance as a base, and extending the trend into the future. When the HR program is implemented, actual performance is compared to the trend line. Any improvement in performance over what the trend-line predicted can then be reasonably attributed to the HR program. While this is not an exact process, it provides a reasonable estimation of the impact of the HR program.

Figure 8 shows an example of trend-line analysis taken from the shipping department of a large distribution company.[11] The percent reflects the level of actual shipments compared to scheduled shipments. Data is presented before and after a team-based structure was implemented. As shown in the figure, there was an upward trend of the data prior to implementing the team structure.

Although the team program apparently had a dramatic effect on shipment productivity, the trend line shows that improvement would have continued anyway, based on the trend that had been previously established. It is tempting to measure the improvement by comparing the average six-months shipments prior to the program (87.3%) to the average of six months after the program (94.4%), yielding a 6.9% difference. However, a more accurate comparison is the six-month average after the program compared to the trend line projection (92.3%). In this case, the difference is 2.1%. Using this more modest measure increases the accuracy and credibility of the process in isolating the impact of the HR program.

The trend line is projected directly from the historical data using a computer program, available in many calculators and software packages.

A primary disadvantage of the trend-line approach is that it is not always accurate. This approach assumes that the events that influenced the performance variable prior

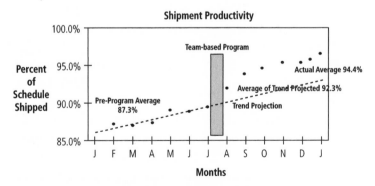

Figure 8. Trend-line analysis

to the program are still in place after the program, except for the implementation of the HR program (i.e., the trends that were established prior to the HR program will continue in the same relative direction.) Also, it assumes that no new influences entered the picture at the time the HR program was implemented. This may not always be the case.

The primary advantage of this approach is that it is simple and inexpensive. If historical data is available, a trend line can quickly be drawn and differences estimated. While not exact, it does provide a very quick assessment of HR's impact.

A more analytical approach to trend-line analysis is a forecasting method that predicts a change in performance variables. This approach provides a mathematical interpretation of the trend-line analysis when other variables enter the situation at the time the HR program is implemented. Output performance is forecasted using a predetermined mathematical relationship with the other influences, and this value is compared to the actual performance. The difference can be attributed to the HR program. Other available references offer more detail about this process.[12]

Participant Estimate of Impact

An easily implemented method for isolating the impact of HR is to obtain information directly from HR program participants. This approach assumes that participants are capable of determining or estimating how much of a performance improvement is related to the HR program.

Because their actions have produced the improvement, participants may have very accurate input on the issue. They should know how much of the change resulted from the implementation of the program. Although it is an estimate, this value will usually have considerable credibility with management because participants are at the center of the change or improvement. Participant estimation is obtained by asking the following series of questions after describing the improvement:

- What factors have contributed to this improvement in performance?

- What percent of this improvement can be attributed to the application and implementation of the HR program?

- What is the basis for this estimate?

- What confidence do you have in this estimate, expressed as a percent?

- Identify other individuals or groups who could estimate this amount

Figure 9 illustrates this approach with an example of one participant's estimations.

Participants who do not provide information on these questions are excluded from the analysis. Also, erroneous, incomplete, and extreme information should be discarded before analysis. To be conservative, the confidence percentage can be factored into the values. The confidence percentage is actually a reflection of the error in the estimate. Thus, an 80% confidence level equates to a potential

Factor Influencing Improvement	Percent of Improvement Caused By	Confidence Expressed as a Percent
1. Training	50%	70%
2. Change in Procedures	10%	80%
3. Adjustment in Performance Standards	10%	50%
4. Revision to Incentive Plan	20%	90%
5. Increased Mangement Attention	10%	50%
6. Other	%	%
Total	100%	

Figure 9.   Example of a participant's estimation

error range of ± 20%. With this approach, the level of confidence is multiplied by the estimate using the lower side of the range. In the example, the participant allocates 50% of the improvement to training, but is only 70% confident with this estimate. The confidence percentage is multiplied by the estimate to develop a usable training factor value of 35%. This adjusted percentage is then multiplied by the actual amount of the improvement (postprogram value minus pre-program value) to isolate the portion attributed to training.

As an added enhancement to this method, management may be asked to review and approve the estimates from participants. For example, in an HR program involving a performance management program for Yellow Freight Systems, a large trucking company, participants estimated the amount of savings that should be attributed to the program.[13] Managers at the next two levels above participants reviewed and approved the estimates. Thus, the managers actually confirmed participants' estimates.

This process has some disadvantages. It is an estimate and, therefore, does not have the accuracy desired by some HR managers. Also, the input data may be unreliable because some participants are incapable of providing these types of estimates. They might not be aware of exactly which factors contributed to the results.

Still, several advantages make this strategy attractive. It is a simple process, easily understood by most participants and by others who review evaluation data. It is inexpensive, takes very little time and analysis, and yields a useful addition to the evaluation process. Estimates originate from a credible source; the individuals who actually produced the improvement. The advantages seem to offset the disadvantages. Isolating the effects of HR will never be precise, and this estimate may be accurate enough for most clients and management groups.

Supervisor and Manager Estimates of the Impact

In lieu of, or in addition to, participant estimates, the participants' supervisors may be asked to provide the extent of HR's role in producing a performance improvement. In some settings, participants' supervisors may be more familiar with the other factors influencing performance. Consequently, they may be better-equipped to provide estimates of impact. The recommended questions to ask supervisors, after describing the improvement attributed to the HR program, are essentially the same ones described for the participant's estimate. Supervisor estimates are also analyzed in the same manner as participant estimates. To be conservative, actual estimates may be adjusted by the confidence percentage.

This approach has the same disadvantages as participant estimates. It is subjective and, therefore, may be viewed with skepticism by senior management. Also, supervisors may be reluctant to participate, or may be incapable of providing accurate impact estimates. The advantages of this approach are similar to the advantages of participant estimation. It is simple and inexpensive, and enjoys an acceptable degree of credibility because it comes directly from the supervisors of those individuals involved in the HR program. When combined with participant estimation, credibility is enhanced. Also, when factored by the level of confidence, its value further increases.

In some cases, upper management may estimate the percent of improvement that should be attributed to the HR program. For example, in Litton Guidance and Control Systems, the results from a self-directed team process were adjusted by management.[14] After considering additional factors, such as technology, procedures, and process changes, which could have contributed to the improvement, senior managers applied a subjective factor, in this case 60%, to represent the portion of the results that should be attributed to the HR program. The 60% factor was developed in a meeting with top managers and therefore had the benefit of group ownership. While this process is very subjective, the input is received from the individuals who often provide or approve funding for the program. Sometimes their level of comfort with the process is the most important consideration.

Using the Strategies

With several strategies available for isolating the impact of HR, selecting the most appropriate strategies for a specific program can be difficult. Some strategies are simple and inexpensive, while others are more time-consuming and costly. When attempting to make the selection decision, several factors should be considered, including feasibility, accuracy, credibility, costs, time required and amount of disruption of work.

Multiple strategies or multiple sources for data input should be considered, because two sources are usually better than one. When multiple sources are utilized, a conservative method to combine the inputs is recommended in order to build acceptance. The target audience should always be provided with explanations of the process and the various subjective factors involved. Multiple sources allow an organization to experiment with different strategies and build confidence with a particular strategy.

Conclusion

This chapter presented a variety of strategies that isolate the effects of HR. The strategies represent the most effective approaches to tackling this issue, and they are utilized by some of the most progressive organizations. Too often, results are reported and linked with HR without any attempt to isolate the portion of results that can be attributed to the HR program. If the HR function is to continue to improve its professional image, as well as to meet its responsibility for obtaining results, this issue must be addressed early in the process.

V.

HR Costs and Data Analysis

F OR SOME HR PROGRAMS, collecting data and isolating the effects of the program is sufficient. However, in other situations, additional analysis is needed. For example, to achieve the ultimate level of evaluation, the return on investment, business impact data (Level 4) must be converted to monetary values and compared to the cost of the HR program or initiative. This calculation will show if there is an economic payoff for the program, measured in monetary terms but often expressed as a ratio or percentage. This chapter focuses on three major issues: converting data to monetary values, tabulating the cost of HR programs and calculating the actual return on investment.

Before considering the specific strategies to convert either hard or soft data to monetary values, it is important to understand the general steps used to convert data in each strategy.

1. Focus on a unit of measure, such as one absence.

2. Determine a value for each unit in monetary terms.

3. Calculate the change in performance data related to the HR program.

4. Determine an annualized amount for the change.

5. Calculate the total value of the annual improvement.

The five-step process is illustrated here with an example taken from a labor-management team-building program at a manufacturing plant.[15] This program was developed and implemented after a needs assessment revealed that a lack of teamwork was causing an excessive number of grievances. The actual number of grievances resolved at Step Two in the grievance process was selected as an output measure.

Step 1: Focus on a Unit of Improvement: One grievance reaching Step Two in the four-step grievance resolution process.

Step 2: Determine a Value for Each Unit: Using internal experts, the labor relations staff, the cost of an average grievance was estimated to be $6,500 when considering time and direct costs [Value (V) = $6,500].

Step 3: Calculate the Change in Performance Data: Six months after the program was completed, total grievances per month reaching Step Two declined by ten. Seven of the ten grievance reductions were related to the program as determined by supervisors (Isolating the Effects of the HR program).

Step 4: Determine an Annual Amount for the Change: Using the six-month value, 7 per month, yields an annual improvement of 84 [Difference in Performance (ΔP)=84].

Step 5: Calculate the Annual Value of the Improvement.
Annual Value = ΔP times V
            = 84 times \$6,500
            = \$546,000

Converting Data to Monetary Values

Several strategies are available to convert data to monetary values. Some are appropriate for a specific type of data or data category, while others can be used with virtually any type of data. The HR staff's challenge is to select the particular strategy that best matches the type of data and situation. Each strategy is presented next, beginning with the most credible approaches.

Converting Output Data to Contribution

When an HR program has produced a change in output, the value of the increased output can usually be determined from the organization's accounting or operating records. For organizations operating on a profit basis, this value is usually the marginal profit contribution of an additional unit of production or unit of service provided. For example, a production team in a major appliance manufacturer is able to boost production of small refrigerators with a work redesign program. The unit of improvement, therefore, is the profit margin of one refrigerator. In organizations that are performance-driven rather than profit-driven, this value is usually reflected in the savings accumulated when an additional unit of output is realized for the same input requirements.

The formulas and calculations used to measure this contribution depend on the organization and its records. Most organizations have this type of data readily available for performance monitoring and goal setting. Managers often use marginal cost statements and sensitivity analyses to pinpoint the value associated with changes in output. If the data is not available, the HR staff should initiate or coordinate the development of appropriate values, or use another strategy.

Calculating the Cost of Quality

Quality is critical, and its cost is an important measure in most manufacturing and service firms. Because many HR programs are designed to improve quality, the

HR staff must locate a monetary value for the improvement for certain quality measures. With some quality measures, the task is easy. For example, if quality is measured with a defect rate, the value of the improvement is the cost to repair or replace the product.

Defective products, spoiled raw materials, and discarded paperwork are all the results of poor quality. This scrap and waste translates directly into a monetary value. For example, in a production environment, the cost of a defective product is the total cost incurred up to the point when the mistake is identified, minus the salvage value.

Employee mistakes and errors can cause expensive rework. The most costly rework occurs when a product is delivered to a customer and must be returned for correction. While cost of rework includes both labor and direct costs, the most expensive element of poor quality is customer dissatisfaction. In some cases, mistakes can result in lost business. Customer dissatisfaction is difficult to quantify, and attempts to arrive at a monetary value may be impossible using direct methods. Usually the judgment and expertise of sales, marketing, or quality managers are the best sources for measuring the monetary impact of dissatisfaction. These and other strategies discussed later in this chapter may be more appropriate for measuring the cost of customer dissatisfaction.

Developing Time Savings

Reduction in employee time is a common objective for HR programs. In a team environment, a program may enable the team to perform tasks in a shorter time frame, or with fewer people. On an individual basis, time management programs are designed to help professional, sales, supervisory, and managerial employees save time in performing daily tasks. The value of the time saved is an important measure of the program's success, and calculating this conversion is a relatively easy process.

The most obvious time savings are from labor reduction costs in performing work. The monetary savings is found by multiplying the hours saved by the average wage per hour. For example, after attending a time management HR program called *Priority Manager,* each participant estimates an average time savings of seventy-four minutes per day, worth $31.25 per day or $7,500 per year.[16] This time savings was based on the average salary plus benefits for the typical participant.

The average wage with a percent added for employee benefits will suffice for most calculations. However, employee time may be worth more. For example, additional costs in maintaining an employee (office space, furniture, telephone, utilities, computers, secretarial support, and other overhead expenses) could be included in the average labor cost. Thus, the average wage rate may quickly escalate to a large number. However, the conservative approach is to use salary plus employee benefits.

A word of caution is in order when the time savings are developed. Savings are only realized when the amount of time saved translates into a cost reduction or profit contribution. If an HR program results in a savings in manager time, a monetary value is realized only if the manager used the additional time in a productive way.

If a team-based program generates a new process that eliminates several hours of work each day, the actual savings will be realized only if there is a cost savings from a reduction in employees or a reduction in overtime pay. Therefore, an important preliminary step in developing time savings is to determine if a "true" savings will be realized.

Using Historical Cost

Sometimes an organization's records contain the value (or cost) of a measure of a unit of improvement. This strategy involves identifying the appropriate records and tabulating the actual cost components for the item in question. For example, a large construction firm implemented a program to improve safety performance. The program improved several safety-related performance measures, ranging from OSHA fines to total worker compensation costs. Examining the company's records using one year of data, the HR staff calculated the average cost for each safety measure.

Using Internal and External Experts' Input

When faced with converting soft data items for which historical records are not available, it might be feasible to consider input from experts on the processes. With this approach, internal experts provide the cost (or value) of one unit of improvement. Individuals who have knowledge of the situation and the respect of the management group are often the best prospects for expert input. These experts must understand the processes and be willing to provide both estimates and the assumptions used in arriving at the estimates. When requesting input from these individuals, it is best to explain the full scope of what is needed, providing as many specifics as possible. Most experts have their own methodology to develop this value.

When internal experts are not available, external experts can be sought. External experts must be selected based on their experience with the unit of measure. Fortunately, many experts are available who work directly with important measures such as employee attitudes, customer satisfaction, turnover, absenteeism, and grievances. They are often willing to provide estimates of the cost (or value) of these items.

Using Values from External Databases

For some soft data items, it may be appropriate to use estimates of the cost (or value) of one unit based on the research of others. This strategy taps external databases that contain studies and research projects focusing on the cost of data items. Fortunately, many databases are available that report cost studies of a variety of data items related to HR programs. Industry, trade association, government, and research databases are sometimes available, frequently through the Internet. Data is available on the cost of turnover, absenteeism, grievances, accidents, and even customer satisfaction. The difficulty lies in finding a database with studies or research efforts for a situation similar to the program under evaluation. Ideally, the data would come from a similar setting in the same industry, but that is not always possible. Sometimes data on all industries or organizations would be sufficient, perhaps with an adjustment to fit the industry under consideration.

Using Estimates from Participants and Supervisors

In some situations, program participants estimate the value of a soft data improvement. This strategy is appropriate when participants are capable of providing estimates of the cost (or value) of the unit of measure improved by the HR program. When using this approach, participants should be provided with clear instructions, along with examples of the type of information needed. The advantage of this approach is that the individuals closest to the improvement are often capable of providing the most reliable estimates of its value.

In some situations, participants may be incapable of placing a value on the improvement. Their work may be so far removed from the output of the process that they cannot reliably provide estimates. In these cases, the team leaders, supervisors, or managers may be capable of providing estimates. Consequently, they may be asked to provide a value for a unit of improvement linked to the program. In other situations, supervisors can be asked to review and approve participants' estimates.

Using HR Staff Estimates

The final strategy for converting data to monetary values is to use the estimates of the HR staff. Using all the available information and experience, the staff members most familiar with the situation provide estimates of the value. Although the HR staff may be capable of providing accurate estimates, this approach may be perceived as being biased. It should be used only when other approaches are not available.

Selecting the Appropriate Strategy

With many strategies available, the challenge is to select one or more strategies appropriate to the situation. The following guidelines can determine the proper selection:

- Use the strategy appropriate for the type of data.

- Move from most accurate to least accurate strategies.

- Consider availability and convenience when selecting a strategy.

- When estimates are sought, use the source who has the broadest perspective on the issue.

- Use multiple strategies when feasible.

- Minimize the amount of time required to select and implement the appropriate strategy.

Accuracy and Credibility of Data

When data is presented to selected target audiences, credibility will be an issue. The degree to which the target audience believes the data will be influenced by factors such as reputation, motive, methodology, assumptions, type of data and scope of analysis.

Collectively, these factors influence the credibility of an impact study and provide a framework from which to develop a summary report. Thus, the following key points are suggested for an HR impact study:

- Use the most credible and reliable source for estimates.

- Present the material in an unbiased, objective way.

- Fully explain the methodology used throughout the process, preferably on a step-by-step basis.

- Define the assumptions made in the analysis, and compare them to assumptions made in other similar studies.

- Consider factoring or adjusting output values when they appear to be unrealistic.

- Use hard data whenever possible and combine with soft data if available.

- Keep the scope of the analysis very narrow. Conduct the impact study with one or more groups of participants in the program, instead of all participants or all employees.

Cost Strategies

Capturing costs is challenging because the figures must be accurate, reliable, and realistic. Although most organizations develop HR costs with much more ease than the monetary value of the benefits, the actual cost of an HR function is often an elusive figure even in some of the best organizations. While the total HR direct budget is usually a number that is easily developed, it is more difficult to determine the specific costs of an HR program, including the indirect costs related to it. Today there is more pressure than ever before to report all HR costs, or what is referred to as *fully-loaded costs*. This takes the cost profile beyond the direct cost of HR programs and includes the cost of the time required for everyone to be involved in the programs. Fortunately, several reports can assist in this effort.[17]

The Danger of Costs without Benefits

It is sometimes dangerous to communicate the costs of an HR program or initiative without presenting benefits. Unfortunately, many organizations have fallen into this trap for years. Because costs can easily be collected, they are presented to management in all types of ingenious ways, such as cost of the program, cost per employee, and cost per day. While these may be helpful for efficiency comparisons, it may be troublesome to present them without benefits. When most executives review the costs of an HR program, one question comes to mind: What benefit was received from the program? This is a typical management reaction, particularly when costs are perceived to be very high. Because of this, some organizations have developed a policy of not communicating HR cost data from a program or initiative unless the benefits can be captured and presented along with the costs. Even if the benefits are subjective and intangible, they are included with the cost data. This helps to balance both issues.

Typical Cost Categories

The most important task is defining which specific costs are included in a tabulation of HR program costs. This task involves decisions by the HR staff, sometimes with input from management. If appropriate, the finance and accounting staff may need to approve the list.

Usually all costs related to a program are captured and expensed to that program. However, three categories are usually prorated over several sessions of the same program. *Needs assessment, design and development* and *acquisition* all represent significant costs that should be prorated over the shelf life of the HR program. With a conservative approach, the shelf life of the program should be very short. Some organizations will consider one year of operation for the program, others may consider two or three years. If there is some question about the specific time period to be used in the proration formula, the finance and accounting staff should be consulted.

When presenting participant salaries and staff associated with programs, the employee benefits factor should be included. This number is usually well-known in the organization and is used in other costing formulas. It represents the cost of all employee benefits expressed as a percent of base salaries. In some organizations this value is as high as 50–60%. In others, it may be as low as 25–30%. The average in the United States is 38%.[18]

Costing a Needs Assessment

One of the most often overlooked items is the cost of conducting a needs assessment and analysis. In some programs this cost is zero because the program is implemented without examining the need. However, as more organizations focus increased attention on needs assessment and analysis, this item will become a more significant cost in the future. All costs associated with the needs assessment should be captured to the fullest extent possible. The total costs are usually prorated over the life of the program.

Design and Development Costs

One of the more significant items is the cost of designing and developing the HR program. These costs include internal HR staff time in both design and development, and the purchase of supplies, videos, CD-ROM's, and other materials directly related to the program. It also includes the use of consultants. As with needs assessment costs, design and development costs are usually prorated, perhaps using the same time frame.

Acquisition Costs

In lieu of development costs, many organizations purchase programs to use directly or in a modified format. The acquisition costs for these programs include the purchase price for the materials, licensing agreements, and any other costs associated with the right to use the program. These acquisition costs should also be prorated.

Delivery and Implementation Costs

Usually the largest segment of HR program costs are those associated with delivery and implementation. Five major categories are included:

- Salaries of coordinators and facilitators

- Program materials and fees

- Travel, lodging and meals

- Facilities and work space used in the program

- Participants' salaries and benefits for the time involved in the HR program

- Time for others involved in the program

Operations/Maintenance

The costs of maintaining the HR program on a continuing basis should be included. This category includes ongoing expenses, supplies, materials, and technology charges to keep the program operational.

Evaluation

Usually the total evaluation cost is included in the program costs to compute the fully loaded cost. The costs of developing the evaluation strategy, designing instruments, collecting data, analyzing data, and reporting the results are included. Cost categories include time, materials, purchased instruments, and surveys.

HR Overhead

A final charge is the cost of overhead, those costs in the HR function not directly related to a particular program or charged to other programs. The overhead category represents any HR department cost not considered in the previous calculations. Typical items include the cost of clerical support, the departmental office expenses, salaries of HR managers, and other fixed costs. An estimate will usually suffice for this value.

The Benefit/Cost Ratio

One of the earliest methods developed for evaluating HR investments is the benefit/cost ratio (BCR). This method compares the benefits of the HR program to the costs of the program. In formula form, the ratio is:

$$BCR = \frac{\text{HR Program Benefits}}{\text{HR Program Costs}}$$

In simple terms, the BCR compares the annual economic benefits of the program to the cost of the program. A BCR of one means that the benefits equal the costs. A BCR of two, usually written as 2:1, indicates that for each dollar spent on the program, two dollars were returned as benefits. For example, a total-quality management program, designed for managers and supervisors, was implemented at an electric and gas utility.[19] In a follow-up evaluation, action planning and business performance monitoring were used to capture benefits. The first year payoff for the program was $1,077,750. The total fully-loaded implementation costs were $215,500. Calculating the ratio:

$$BCR = \frac{\$1,077,750}{\$215,500} = 5:1$$

For every one dollar invested in this program, five dollars in benefits were returned.

Return on Investment

Perhaps the most appropriate formula for evaluating HR investments is net program benefits divided by cost, or *return on investment* (ROI). The ratio is usually expressed as a percent when the fractional values are multiplied by 100. In formula form:

$$ROI\% = \frac{\text{Net HR Program Benefits}}{\text{HR Program Costs}} \times 100$$

Net benefits are program benefits minus program costs. The ROI value is related to the BCR by a factor of one. For example, a BCR of 2.45 is the same as an the ROI value of 145%. This formula is essentially the same as ROI in other types of investments. For example, when a firm builds a new plant, the ROI is developed by dividing annual earnings by the investment. The annual earnings is comparable to net benefits (annual benefits minus the cost). The investment is comparable to HR program costs, which represent the investment in the program.

An ROI on an HR investment of 50% means that the costs are recovered and an additional 50% of the costs are reported as "earnings." For example, Magnavox Electron-ics Systems Company conducted an 18-week literacy program for entry-level electrical and mechanical assemblers.[20] The results of the program were impressive. Productivity and quality alone yielded an annual value of $321,600. The total fully-loaded costs for the program were $38,233. Thus, the return on investment becomes

$$\text{ROI\%} = \frac{\$\,321{,}600 - \$\,38{,}233}{\$\,38{,}233} \times 100 = 741\%$$

For each dollar invested, Magnavox received $7.40 in return after the cost of the program had been recovered.

Using the ROI formula essentially places HR invest-ments on a level playing field with other investments using the same formula and similar concepts. The ROI calcula-tion is easily understood by key management and financial executives who regularly use ROI with other investments.

While there are no generally accepted standards at the present time, some organizations establish a minimum requirement, or *hurdle rate,* for an ROI in an HR program. An ROI minimum of 25% is set by some organizations. This target value is usually above the percentage required for other types of investments. The rationale: The ROI process for HR is still relatively new and often involves some subjective input, including estimates. Because of that, a higher standard is required or suggested, with 25% being the desired figure for these organizations.

Measuring the ROI	Key Variables
A New Recruiting Source	Costs, Yield, Early Turnover
A Revised Orientation Program	Early Turnover, Training time
Training Programs	Productivity, Sales, Quality, Time, Costs, Customer Service, Turnover, Absenteeism, Employee Satisfaction
Career Development Program	Turnover, Employee Satisfaction, Organizational Commitment
Skill-based Pay	Labor Costs, Turnover, Absenteeism
A Wellness/Fitness Center	Turnover, Medical Costs, Absenteeism
A Labor-Management Cooperation Program	Grievances, Absenteeism
Safety Incentive Plan	Accident Frequency Rates, Accident Severity Rates
Associate Relations Program	Turnover, Employee Satisfaction
A Gainsharing Plan	Production Costs, Productivity, Turnover
Total Quality Management	Defects, Rework, Response Time
Self-Directed Teams	Productivity, Quality, Customer Satisfaction, Turnover, Absenteeism, Employee Satisfaction

Figure 10.   Typical ROI studies

The ROI process has been used with a variety of HR programs and with excellent results. Figure 10 shows the range of studies conducted by one consulting organization.[21] Specific variables for the monetary values are also included.

Because of the complexity and sensitivity of the ROI process, caution is needed when developing, calculating, and communicating the return on investment. Implementation of the ROI process is a very important goal of many HR departments. A few issues should be addressed to keep the process from going astray:

- The ROI process is more appropriate for HR programs for which a needs assessment has been conducted.

- The ROI analysis should always include one or more strategies for isolating the effects of the HR program.

- When making estimates, use the most reliable and credible sources.

- Take a conservative approach when developing both benefits and costs.

- Use caution when comparing the ROI in HR with other financial returns.

- Involve management in developing the return.

- Approach sensitive and controversial issues with caution.

- Teach others the methods for calculating the return.

- Do not boast about a high return.

- Do not try to use ROI on every program, only a few critical programs.

Intangible Measures

Intangible measures are often monitored after the HR program has been implemented, and although they are not converted to monetary values, they are still very important in the evaluation process. While the range of intangible measures is almost unlimited, following are the most common variables often linked with HR programs:

- Attitude survey data

- Organizational commitment

- Climate survey data

- Employee complaints

- Grievances

- Discrimination complaints

- Stress reduction

- Employee turnover

- Employee absenteeism

- Employee tardiness

- Employee transfers

- Customer satisfaction survey data

- Customer complaints
- Customer response time
- Teamwork
- Cooperation
- Conflict
- Decisiveness
- Communication

Conclusion

In conclusion, organizations are attempting to be more creative and aggressive when developing the monetary benefits of HR programs and initiatives. Progressive HR managers are no longer satisfied with reporting business performance results from HR programs. Instead, they are taking additional steps to convert business results data to monetary values and compare them with the program's fully-loaded costs. The result is the ultimate level of evaluation, the return on investment. This chapter presented strategies to convert business results to monetary values, tabulate costs of programs, and calculate the return on investment. Two basic approaches for calculating the return were presented; the ROI formula and the benefit/cost ratio.

VI.

SHIFTING THE PARADIGM: IMPLEMENTATION ISSUES

THE BEST-DESIGNED EVALUATION PROCESS, model, technique, or framework is worthless unless it is integrated efficiently and effectively into the organization. The measurement and evaluation processes presented in this book will fail, even in the best organizations, if they are not integrated into routine activities and strategies, and fully accepted and supported by those who should make it work in the organization. This chapter focuses on the critical issues involved in implementing a comprehensive HR measurement process, showing how an organization should position measurement and evaluation as an essential component of HR.

Leadership

As a first step in the process, one or more individuals, or team, should be designated as the internal leader or champion for measurement and evaluation. As in most change efforts, someone must take the responsibility for ensuring that the process is implemented successfully. This leader or team understands the process best and sees the vast potential for the HR contribution. More important, this leader is willing to show and teach others.

In preparation for this assignment, individuals usually obtain special training to build specific skills and knowledge in the ROI process. The role of the implementation leader is very broad and serves a variety of specialized purposes. Ten specific skill sets are identified with the success of a comprehensive measurement and evaluation implementation:[22]

- Planning for measurement and evaluation

- Collecting data

- Isolating the effects of HR programs

- Converting data to monetary values

- Monitoring HR program costs

- Analyzing data, including calculating the ROI

- Presenting evaluation data

- Implementing the process

- Providing internal consulting

- Teaching others the process

It is necessary to build the appropriate skills to tackle this challenging assignment.

Responsibilities

Determining responsibilities is a critical issue because confusion can result when individuals are unclear of their specific assignments. Responsibilities apply to two HR groups. The first is the measurement and evaluation responsibility for the entire HR staff. It is important for all of those involved in developing, coordinating, and analyzing HR programs to have some responsibility for measurement and evaluation. Typical responsibilities include:

- Ensuring that the needs assessment includes specific business impact measures

- Developing specific application objectives and business impact objectives for each program

- Focusing the content of HR programs on performance improvement or cost savings

- Keeping HR program participants focused on application and impact objectives

- Communicating the rationale and reasons for evaluation

- Assisting in follow-up activities to capture application and business impact data

- Providing technical assistance for data collection, data analysis and reporting

- Designing instruments and plans for data collection and analysis

- Presenting evaluation data to a variety of groups

While it is inappropriate to have each member of the HR staff involved in all of these activities, individuals should have at least one or more responsibilities as part of their routine job duties. This assignment of responsibility keeps the process from being disjointed and separate from other activities. More important, it brings accountability to those who develop and coordinate the programs.

The second responsibility is the technical support function. Depending on the size of the HR staff, it may be helpful to establish a group of technical experts who provide assistance with measurement and evaluation. When this group is established, it must be clear that the experts are not there to relieve others of evaluation responsibilities, but to supplement technical expertise. Typical technical support responsibilities include:

- Designing data collection instruments

- Providing assistance for developing an evaluation strategy

- Analyzing data, including specialized statistical analyses

- Interpreting results and making specific recommendations

- Developing an evaluation report or case study to communicate overall results

- Providing technical support in any phase of the ROI process

Policies and Procedures

Another important element of implementation is revising (or developing) the organization's policy concerning measurement and evaluation, often a part of overall HR policy and practice. The policy statement contains information developed specifically for measurement and evaluation, usually with the input of the HR staff and key managers or clients. Typical topics include adopting the five-level model presented in this book, requiring Level 3 and Level 4 objectives in some or all HR programs, and defining responsibilities for measurement and evaluation.

Policy statements are very important because they provide guidance and direction for the HR staff and others who work closely with evaluation. They help the group to establish goals for evaluation. Goals enable the HR staff to focus on the improvements needed at specific evaluation levels. With this framework, each HR program, initiative, or function has an evaluation plan, detailing which levels of evaluation will be conducted.

Policy statements also provide an opportunity to communicate basic requirements and standards regarding HR accountability. More than anything else, they serve as a learning tool for teaching others, especially when they are developed collaboratively.

Procedures for measurement and evaluation are important for showing how to utilize the tools and techniques, guiding the design process, providing consistency in the process, ensuring that appropriate methods are used and placing the proper emphasis on validity.

Procedures are more technical than policy statements and often contain detailed guidelines showing how the process is actually undertaken and developed. They often include forms, instruments, and tools necessary for facilitating the process.

HR Staff Preparation

One group that will usually resist evaluation is the HR staff. They must design, develop, coordinate and facilitate HR programs. These staff members often see evaluation as an unnecessary intrusion into their responsibilities, absorbing precious time, and stifling their freedom to be creative.

One reason for HR staff resistance is that the effectiveness of their programs will be fully exposed, placing their reputation on the line. They may have a fear of failure. To overcome this, measurement and evaluation should be positioned as a tool for learning, and not as a tool for evaluating HR staff performance, at least during its early years of implementation. HR staff members will not be interested in developing a process that will be used against them.

HR program stakeholders can learn as much from failures as successes. If a program is not working, it is best to find out quickly and make adjustments. If a program is ineffective and not producing the desired results, it will eventually be known to clients and/or the management group, if they are not aware of it already. Lack of results will cause managers to become less supportive of HR. If adjustments are made quickly when the weaknesses of programs are identified, not only will effective programs be developed, but the credibility and respect for the HR function will be enhanced.

The HR staff will usually have inadequate skills in measurement and evaluation and thus will need to develop expertise. Measurement and evaluation are not usually a formal part of their preparation. Consequently, each HR staff member must be provided with training to learn how the process works, step by step. In addition, staff members must know how to develop an evaluation strategy plan, collect and analyze data from the evaluation, and interpret results from data analysis.

ROI Projects

The first tangible evidence of the ROI process may be initiation of the first project for an ROI calculation. Selecting a program for ROI analysis is a critical issue, because only specific types of programs should be selected for a comprehensive, detailed analysis. Typical criteria are programs that:

- Involve large target audiences

- Are expected to have a long life

- Are important to overall strategic objectives

- Are expensive

- Have high visibility

- Have a comprehensive needs assessment

Using these, or similar criteria, the HR staff must select the appropriate programs to consider for an ROI project. Ideally, management should concur with, or approve, the criteria.

The next major step is determining how many projects to undertake initially and in which particular areas. A small number of initial projects is recommended, perhaps three or four programs. The selected programs may represent the functional areas of the business such as operations, sales, finance, engineering, and information technology. Another approach is to select programs representing functional areas of HR, such as recruiting, employment, training, management development, compensation, compliance and employee relations. It is important to select a manageable number so the process can be implemented with existing resources.

Management Training

Perhaps no group is more important to measurement and evaluation than the management team that must allocate resources and support HR programs. In addition, they often provide input and assistance with the process. Specific ways to collaborate with the management team should be carefully planned and executed.

One approach is to conduct a workshop, "The Manager's Role in Human Resources." Varying in duration from half a day to two days, this practical workshop shapes critical skills and changes perceptions to enhance the support for HR. Managers leave the workshop with an improved perception of the impact of HR and a clearer understanding of their HR roles. More important, they often have a renewed commitment to make HR more effective in their organization.

Monitoring Progress and Communicating Results

A final part of the implementation process is monitoring the overall progress made and communicating the results at specific intervals. Although it is an often overlooked part of the process, an effective communication plan can help keep the implementation on target and let others know what HR is accomplishing for the organization.

The implementation plan (if there is one) includes a variety of key events or milestones appropriate for progress reporting. Routine progress reports need to be developed to present the status and progress of these events or milestones. Reports are usually developed at six-month intervals. Two target audiences, the HR staff and senior managers, are critical for progress reporting. The entire HR staff should be kept informed of the progress, and senior managers need to know the extent to which measurement and evaluation is being implemented and how it is working in the organization.

The results from an impact study must be reported to a variety of target audiences. The typical impact study report provides background information, explains the processes used and, most important, presents the results. Reaction, learning and implementation results are presented first. Business impact results are presented next, followed by the actual ROI calculation, if applicable. Finally, other issues are covered along with the intangible benefits.

Conclusion

In summary, implementation of a comprehensive measurement and evaluation process is critical. If not approached in a systematic, planned way, the process will not become an integral part of HR, and the accountability of HR programs will be lacking. This chapter presented the major issues that must be considered to ensure that implementation is smooth and uneventful. The result should be a complete integration of measurement and evaluation into routine HR processes.

VII.

Looking Ahead

W E MENTIONED EARLIER that staff departments have typically been viewed as expense centers. This view developed as everyone bought the idea and began to manage staff functions that way. Cutting the cost of staff functions has long been a primary objective. With every downturn in the business cycle, staff groups are decimated. In many cases this has been proven to be penny-wise and pound-foolish.

Staff departments play a vital role when they connect themselves to the SQP objectives of their line customers. A better way to manage staff is to view them as potential contributors to profit. If you asked yourself what could we do in human resources to contribute to profit, you would think of several ways to do that. This book has described many tools and processes for contributing tangible value to the enterprise.

The HR Star

As companies adjust to the new forces of the twenty-first century, HR has to find a basic model for staying in alignment with its customers. In times of great flux and uncertainty, the best approach is usually the simplest and closest to bedrock management. Basically, the human resources function has five responsibilities: planning, staffing, paying, developing and retaining human capital. The HR Star (see Figure 11), reveals how the five functions are interdependent.

Workforce Planning

Workforce planning is making a comeback. The main human capital activity from the late 1980s through the mid 1990s was staff reduction. By 1997, some people

Figure 11.   HR star

began to wonder how in the world they were going to compete when they didn't have enough of the necessary skills resident in the workforce. As the economy boomed, recruiting heated up and competition for technical skills became a pitched battle. Over time, a shortage of reliable workers at all levels became a central problem. The more farsighted looked up from the daily struggle and decided they had to consider the future as well as the present. This led them back to workforce planning (WFP).

Let's face it, WFP is tedious. It requires developing a vast amount of data on the competencies of the current workforce. Just setting up the system and getting agreement on definitions and levels of skills can be drudgery. A small number of companies have persevered and developed a thorough description of their skills profile. Others are studying ways to do it that won't be so time-consuming.

No matter what size your organization is, you have to look ahead to your future skills profile. If you devote a reasonable amount of time to planning, you will have it returned in reduced hiring time and cost, lower training costs for new employees, and probably higher productivity through a more stable and motivated workforce.

Staffing

Hiring during periods of sustained high growth becomes an all-consuming task. The only thing that will make it easier is having good data on the results of your current practices. Doesn't it make sense that if you know how much it costs, how long it takes, and the quality and availability of each of your major sources, you can do a better job? The classic excuse is, "I don't have time to analyze what I am doing; I'm too busy." As they say, those who ignore history are condemned to repeat its mistakes. The same is true here. A little time devoted now to measurement and analysis will pay back later in reduced workload and lower stress for all—not to mention reduced cost.

Paying

Pay covers wages, salaries and benefits—the total cash investment in human assets. We can do a better job of managing that investment if we look at it from a resource viewpoint. First, we should determine what percent of revenue the business conditions dictate to be the most efficient level of pay. That is, how much of every dollar we take in should we invest in human assets? This is analyzed through a pyramid model, shown in Figure 12.

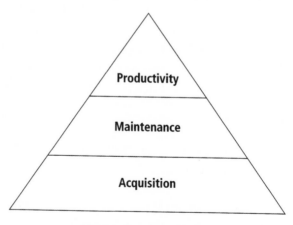

Figure 12. Pay pyramid

How much of your total compensation dollar can and should you invest in initial pay levels for new hires, to maintain and retain skilled personnel, and to motivate them to be productive? There are many options here. The decision should be based on management's philosophy regarding human value added and the company's ability to pay. By looking at the question from the standpoint of the pyramid you might get new insights.

Developing

Employee development is no longer an option. There simply aren't enough skills in the national labor pool to support the growth curve into the next decade. The make/buy decision has been preempted by a lack of supply. The national investment in training has been increasing at a steady 5% per year, compounded since the early years of the decade. The key business issue now is where to spend development dollars. Basic skills, management competencies and executive development are all priorities. Despite the obvious basic skills shortage, we would suggest that the biggest opportunity is in executive leadership development. A study of 600 companies across many industries revealed a belief that leadership in the twenty-first century will require new skills and insights.[23] In the final analysis, if we don't develop effective leaders, we won't have to worry about basic skills because we will be out of business.

Retaining

When the supply is limited, a wise strategy is to pay attention to keeping what you have. Consider what it costs to lose a skilled employee: the direct costs of termination, hiring a replacement, vacancy costs and learning curve loss. These add up to more than one year's pay and benefits for an exempt person. Add to that the external costs in unhappy and lost customers, and the number goes out of sight. One study claims that the costs of losing an effective salesperson can take up to three years to recover.[24]

The most common cause of voluntary termination is not pay or opportunity elsewhere. That only tips the scale in favor of leaving. An ongoing study now covering over 20,000 cases of voluntary turnover has revealed that 80% of the cases were triggered by problems with a supervisor, working conditions, and perceived lack of career opportunities. Work conditions related to flexibility and respect for the worker's personal needs. Actually, this is good news. You might not be able to outbid someone for your valued employee, but you certainly can do something about supervisory skills, working conditions, and career opportunity.

Working Cross-Functionally

In our combined forty years of human resources experience, we have seldom seen HR departments in which all the sections work as one unit. The intention might be there, but few HR directors have developed management systems that induce everyone to work for the greater good of HR.

There are natural connections across sections of HR that are often ignored. Following are some examples:

- Hiring and Training: The buy it or make it question should be discussed among all HR sections and, most importantly, the staffing and development people.

- Paying and Retaining: Employee-relations people, if they are doing their job, can feed a good deal of information to the compensation and benefits group about employee attitudes toward pay and benefits.

- Paying and Benefits: In many large companies the compensation and benefits people are disconnected. If they communicate effectively they can find ways to maximize the total return on investment in human assets.

- Planning–Staffing–Paying–Developing–Retaining: The human assets of the organization need to be reviewed holistically. People care as much about personal growth as pay. They are turned on and off by policies in all five areas of the HR star. The best solution is usually found in a five-point view.

Monitoring the Effects of a Collaborative Approach

When HR professionals work with their managers, customers and their professional colleagues, the results are usually measurable. They can trace the effects of their work in several ways:

- Lower hiring costs
- Faster time filling jobs
- Higher-quality hires
- Higher levels of retention
- Lower development costs
- Higher levels of productivity

To set up a valid and reliable measurement program, all you need to do is have clear targets in mind at the beginning of the process. Then, you build a case for the relationship between your recommended action steps and effects on business unit processes. It is much easier than you think. This book has provided many examples to guide you.

The Top Ten Measures of HR's Effectiveness

There is no end to the number of actions and results that can be measured. What to measure depends on what is important to the organization. As a generalization, we would say that the following are among the most important for most companies:

10. *Healthcare cost per employee.* The aging workforce will put added pressure on healthcare cost containment. Until the healthcare industry shakes

out a new, more efficient delivery process, this single large cost should be monitored.

9. *Pay and benefits as a percentage of operating expense.* Downsizings or rightsizings are aimed at reducing the company's operating expenses. This metric is one way to see if people cost is dropping at the same rate as other expenses.

8. *Cost per hire.* The quality of the hire is more important than the cost. Nevertheless, it is quite useful to track hiring cost. The standard formula that applies in almost all cases is: advertising + agency fees + employee referrals + travel of applicants and staff + relocation + the cost of the internal recruiter . . . plus 10% to cover all other related costs.

7. *Return on training.* One great challenging issue is the calculation of return on investment in training. Ironically, although trainers are concerned that if they try to show ROI it won't be there, training almost always shows a huge ROI.

6. *Turnover rate.* Retention of key employees is probably the biggest challenge in human asset management today. Organizations need to know who is leaving, at what point during their period of employment are most people leaving and, of course, the reasons for leaving. This data can be used to dramatically cut unwanted turnover.

5. *Turnover cost.* The key issue in turnover is not only that skills are lost, but so is a lot of money. There are four components of turnover cost: termination, replacement, vacancy, and learning curve loss. Losing as few as six skilled exempt persons can cost a company over $1,000,000!

4. *Time to fill jobs.* Filling jobs quickly—with quality people—is a critical need. HR has more opportunity to influence this result than any other function. Time should be measured in calendar days.

3. *Return on human capital invested.* For decades the question of the value of an employee has been debated. Here is a simple solution: Take revenue and subtract operating expense less the cost of pay and benefits. This "adjusted profit" figure divided by the cost of pay and benefits shows the rate of return on people.

2. *Human value added.* Do the same calculation as Return on Human Capital Invested, but divide that adjusted profit figure by the number of full-time equivalent employees and contract workers. This shows the leverage that people have on profitability expressed as adjusted profit dollars per person.

1. *The one that means the most to your boss.* Be honest: Your survival and advancement are largely dependent on your boss. It makes sense to show that you have met or exceeded his/her needs.

Human resources department costs and staff ratios are not included in the Top Ten. That is because they are of lesser importance. Form follows function. You establish the size and cost of the HR function based on the organization's needs and expectations from HR. Budget and staff is not the driving force of an effective, business partnering HR department. A clear vision of a value adding purpose separates the best from the rest.

How To Contribute Tomorrow

Anticipation is a much-appreciated skill in an uncertain world. HR must develop the insights needed to tell its management customers what is coming tomorrow. This is not magic. Two actions can prepare you:

1. Maintain a broad-based view of the world. The important, driving forces of the marketplace are outside of HR. Information technology, social trends, financial news and competitors' actions are the stuff of prediction. Scan the media and subscribe to an Internet news page. In the space of fifteen minutes a day, you can catch the most important events that will affect the investment in human capital.

2. Prepare the HR staff with business skills. Forget HR skills for the moment and concentrate in three areas: analytic ability, selling skills and interpersonal competence.

The Final Truth

For decades people have been writing about how the human resources function is on the ascendancy, claiming that because human assets or human capital is being recognized as the last great leverage point for business, the human resources function is critical. That is true. What is also true is the evidence that only a small percentage of human resources groups are taking advantage of this opportunity. Witness the fact that many HR managers are now coming from finance, marketing and operations, not from within the HR profession. The message should be clear. The opportunity to play is here and now. But in order to make the team, HR professionals have to become business professionals as well.

REFERENCES

1. Rifkin, Jeremy. *The End of Work*. New York: G.P. Putnam & Sons, 1995.

2. Bridges, William. *Job Shift*. Reading, MA: Addison Wesley Publishing, 1994.

3. *Human Resource Financial Reports*. Santa Clara, CA: Saratoga Institute, 1991–1997.

4. Stewart, G. Bennett. *The Quest for Value*. New York: Harper Collins, 1991.

5. Fitz-enz, Jac, *Human Value Management*. San Francisco, CA: Jossey-Bass, 1990.

6. Fitz-enz, Jac, *How to Measure Human Resources Management*. New York: McGraw-Hill, 2nd edition, 1995.

7. Treacy, Michael and Fred Wiersema, *The Discipline of Market Leaders*. Reading, MA: Addison Wesley Publishing, 1995.

8. Kirkpatrick, D. L., "Techniques for Evaluating Training Programs," *Evaluating Training Programs*. Alexandria, VA: ASTD, 1975, pp. 1–17.

9. Ferris, Gerald, R. (ed.), *Research in Personnel and Human Resources Management*. Vol. 11, Greenwich, CT: JAI Press, Inc., 1993.

10. Schoeppel, Cynthia, "Turning Down Manager Turnover: Financial Services, Inc." *In Action: Measuring Return on Investment*. Vol. 1, Alexandria, VA: ASTD, 1994, pp. 213–22.

11. Phillips, Jack, J., *Return on Investment in Training and Performance Improvement Programs*. Houston, TX: Gulf Publishing, 1997.

12. Phillips, Jack, J., "Was It the Training?" *Training and Development*. March, 1996, pp. 28–32.

13. Zigon, J., "Performance Management Training," *In Action: Measuring Return on Investment*. Vol. 1, Alexandria, VA: ASTD, 1994, pp. 253–270.

14. Graham, M., K. Bishop, and R. Birdsong, "Self-Directed Work Teams," *In Action: Measuring Return on Investment*. Vol. 1, Alexandria, VA: ASTD, 1994, pp. 105–122.

15. Phillips, Jack J., *Return on Investment in Training and Performance Improvement Programs*. Houston, TX: Gulf Publishing, 1997.

16. Stamp, D., *The Workplace of the Twenty-First Century*. Bellevue, WA: A publication of Priority Management Systems, 1992.

17. Fitz-enz, Jac, (Ed) *Human Resources Effectiveness Report*. Saratoga, CA: Saratoga Institute, 1997.

18. Annual Employee Benefits Report, *National Business*. January, 1996, P. 28.

19. Wescott, R., "Applied Behavior Management Training," *In Action: Measuring Return on Investment.* Vol. 1, Alexandria, VA: ASTD, 1994, pp. 235–252.

20. Ford, D., "Three Rs in the Workplace," *In Action: Measuring Return on Investment.* Vol. 1, Alexandria, VA: ASTD, 1994, pp. 85–104.

21. Phillips, Jack J., *Accountability in Human Resource Management.* Houston, TX: Gulf Publishing, 1996.

22. Phillips, Jack J., *Return on Investment in Training and Performance Improvement Programs.* Houston, TX: Gulf Publishing, 1997.

23. *Leadership Development, A Report by the Saratoga Institute.* New York: American Management Association, January, 1998.

24. Reichheld, Frederick F., *The Loyalty Effect.* Cambridge, MA: HBS Press, 1996.

Further Reading

Fitz-enz, Jac. *Human Value Management*. San Francisco, CA: Jossey-Bass, 1990.

Fitz-enz, Jac. *How to Measure Human Resources Management*. New York: McGraw-Hill, 2nd edition, 1995.

Hussey, David. *Business Driven Resource Management*. Chichester: John Wiley & Sons, Ltd., 1997.

Leadership Development, A Report by the Saratoga Institute. New York: American Management Association, January, 1998.

Phillips, Jack J., *Accountability in Human Resource Management*. Houston, TX: Gulf Publishing, 1996.

Phillips, Jack J., Ed., *Measuring Return on Investment*. Vol. 1 (1994), Vol, 2 (1997), American Society for Training and Development, 1997.

Reichheld, Frederick F., *The Loyalty Effect*. Cambridge, MA: HBS Press, 1996.

Smllansky, Jonathan, *The New HR*. London: International Thomson Business Press, 1997.

Ulrich, Dave. *Human Resources Champions*. Boston: Harvard Business School Publishing, 1996.

ABOUT THE AUTHORS

Jac Fitz-enz is the acknowledged father of human asset benchmarking and evaluation. He formulated and carried out the initial research on human asset measurement in the 1970s at the Saratoga Institute. Since 1977, Dr. Fitz-enz has trained over 40,000 managers in 40 countries on human performance measurement. Through the Institute, Dr. Fitz-enz has served 90 of the Fortune 100 companies, as well as many foreign-based multinational corporations.

He has edited over 20 national reports, and published 100 articles and four books on human performance measurement. The first book, *How to Measure Human Resource Management,* published in 1984, remains the seminal text on quantitative evaluation of human resource operations. Dr. Fitz-enz's second book, *Human Value Management,* won the 1991 SHRM Book of the Year Award. His most recent work, *The Eight Practices of Exceptional Companies,* describes five years of research on 1,000 companies, which yielded the factors common to the top human asset managing companies.

Dr. Fitz-enz leads Saratoga Institute's ongoing multinational research programs on human resources department performance and human asset evaluation. His value measurement work is the principal reference of every major human resource association. Under his guidance, the Saratoga Institute has become the primary worldwide source of human financial benchmarks from twenty countries.

Prior to founding the Saratoga Institute in 1977, Dr. Fitz-enz had twenty years of business experience in several line functions, and held human resource vice presidential positions at Wells Fargo Bank, Imperial Bank and Motorola Computer Systems.

Dr. Jac Fitz-enz, Saratoga Institute, Inc., 3600 Pruneridge Avenue, Santa Clara, California 95051

Dr. Jack Phillips is the global leader in applying the ROI process to human resource programs and initiatives. With over 27 years of corporate experience in five industries (aerospace, textiles, metals, construction materials and banking), he has served as training and development manager at two Fortune 500 firms, senior HR officer at two firms, president of a regional Federal Savings Bank and management professor for a major state university.

In 1992, Dr. Phillips founded Performance Resources Organization (PRO), an international consulting firm specializing in human resources accountability. PRO clients include some of the world's largest and most prestigious organizations, including many Fortune 500 companies. In addition to the U.S.A. and Canada, clients are located in over 20 countries, including England, Belgium, Italy, Germany, Sweden, South Africa, Mexico, Venezuela, Malaysia, Indonesia, Hong Kong, Australia and Singapore.

Dr. Phillips has authored or edited fourteen books in the areas of accountability, performance improvement and human resource management. Titles include *Return*

on Investment in Training and Performance Improvement Programs
(1997), *Accountability in Human Resource Management* (1996),
Handbook of Training Evaluation and Measurement Methods
(3rd edition, 1997), *Measuring Return on Investment* (Volume
2, 1997), *Measuring Return on Investment* (Volume 1, 1994),
which continues to be a No. 1 bestseller, *Conducting Needs
Assessment* (1995), *The Development of a Human Resource
Effectiveness Index* (1988), *Recruiting, Training and Retaining
New Employees* (1987) and *Improving Supervisors Effectiveness*
(1985), which won an award from the Society for Human
Resource Management. He has also written more than
100 articles for professional, business and trade
publications.

With undergraduate degrees in electrical engineering,
physics and mathematics from Southern Polytechnic State
University and Oglethorpe University, Phillips received a
master's degree in Decision Sciences from Georgia State
University and a Ph.D. in Human Resource Management
from the University of Alabama. In 1987, he won the
Yoder-Heneman Personnel Creative Application Award
from the Society for Human Resource Management.

Dr. Jack J. Phillips, Chairman and CEO, Performance
Resources Organization, P. O. Box 380637, Birmingham,
Alabama 35238-0637